P. N. Townend

TOP SHED

A PICTORIAL HISTORY OF KINGS CROSS LOCOMOTIVE DEPOT

LONDON

IAN ALLAN LTD

For Mark and Wendy

First published 1975

ISBN 0 7110 0648 2—107/74

Published by Ian Allan Ltd, Shepperton, Surrey, and printed in the United Kingdom by Biddles Ltd, Guildford, Surrey.

Above: Ivatt ten-wheeled suburban tank No. 1504 standing at Enfield. The old-type rotating square route indicator is visible above the front buffer beam. *(I. Allan collection)*

Title page: The three types of Gresley Pacifics, Classes A4, A3 and A1, outside the Main Line Shed in pre-war days. *(Keystone/British Railways)*

Contents

Introduction   6

1   Construction of the GNR London engine stables   8

2   The Midland Roundhouse   18

3   Developments at the London Depot   24

4   Some of the earlier Top Shed Superintendents   44

5   King's Cross locomotives   50

6   Shed work in the 1950's   72

7   Some diagram and engine working arrangements   98

8   Suburban workings   111

9   Some Specials and Relief Trains   124

10   Living with the Pacifics   136

Appendices:

Allocation of the London Division January 1922   174

Allocation of King's Cross Depot April 1958   175

Introduction

Although I had ridden on Top Shed locomotives on many occasions since I had started my railway career on the LNER in 1941 as a Premium Apprentice in Doncaster Works, I had never actually worked at or visited the depot at King's Cross until 1953. In the spring of 1956 the post of Locomotive Shed Master at King's Cross became vacant and I was promoted from Boston to fill the vacancy.

For most of my life I had known the East Coast Main Line and had been familiar with the LNER locomotives from an early age. In 1935 I was one of an exceedingly large number of spectators who gathered on Doncaster Station for a few minutes after half-past-seven late in September to see and hear the "Silver Jubilee" go north on its first day of entering regular service. Little did I know that twenty-one years later I would be responsible for the maintenance and running of nineteen A4 locomotives at King's Cross Depot.

In this book I have attempted to outline the construction and subsequent development of the depot, which eventually became widely known as Top Shed, from the time the first engine stables were built there in 1850 to the final closure in 1963. Mention has been made of some of the former King's Cross Superintendents and many of the principal locomotive classes which have worked from King's Cross over the years, and a little about the work of these locomotives. Much of what is related in the remainder of the book is concerned with the working arrangements and events which took place between 1956 and 1963 whilst I was responsible for the depot or nearby in the Traffic Manager's Office.

I have endeavoured to avoid writing a detailed history of the locomotives of either the Great Northern Railway or the London & North Eastern Railway, as this has been well covered elsewhere. Some may regret that reference has not been made to more of the exploits of the famous locomotives of the past or the personalities which drove them, but in many of these deeds the depot was not particularly involved.

The illustrations have been chosen to cover as wide a range of King's Cross locomotives as possible, and many of the photographs selected have been taken in the area of the Shed or the Station. The final chapter deals with the Pacifics in rather more detail covering the difficulties experienced with them and how these were largely overcome.

Whilst the five years or so I spent at Top Shed were probably the hardest I have experienced, I am glad that I had the opportunity to be associated with the depot in all its vicissitudes whilst steam traction was still at its peak on the Great Northern Main Line. Although many people, including the author, have regretted the passing of the steam locomotive, after spending a number of years trying to overcome some of the problems associated with their operation, the end was inevitable. People generally were not prepared to accept the dirt, grime and smoke associated with steam traction and there were many menial unpleasant tasks which were required to be carried out in primitive conditions at depots which few men really wanted to do. Nevertheless, the change over to diesel traction was made much more easily by having many of the finest steam locomotives in the country allocated to King's Cross. I am specially grateful for all the assistance given to me by the many grades of railway staff at King's Cross without which the results achieved could never have been attained. The views expressed, however, are entirely my own.

A considerable amount of the historical information has been found in the Public Records Office (former BRB Archives) at Porchester Road, but much has also been gleaned from the *Locomotive Magazine,* the *Railway Gazette,* the *LNER Magazine,* and many others published over the years. I am grateful to my railway colleagues, including those at Euston and Liverpool Street, for allowing me access to their bound volumes, and to many individuals who have given me every encouragement and much assistance in the writing of this book. My special thanks are due to Mrs. Goddard for allowing me to reproduce the letter addressed to her father written by Sir Nigel Gresley in his own hand, to David Somers for redrawing the first plan of the depot and the Gresley middle big end, and to Mrs. Ada Turp who was herself employed at Top Shed for many years and still interprets my writing.

Photographs are acknowledged individually in the text. The print of the Locomotive Hall at King's Cross is reproduced by permission of the London Borough of Camden from the Local History Collections.

P. N. Townend

1

Construction of the GNR London engine stables

The original Great Northern Railway engine stables at London were built in 1850, three-quarters of a mile to the north-west of the present King's Cross station.

A temporary terminal off Maiden Lane, now known as York Way, was brought into use from August 1850, and the present main-line station at King's Cross was not opened for traffic until October 1852. The original locomotive depot was nearer to and on the same ground level as the early temporary London terminus, but King's Cross station was constructed at a lower level in order that the line could pass underneath the Regent's Canal to reach it. The terminal was situated on the south side of the canal, facing on to the New Road from Paddington to Islington, later known as Euston Road. Little demolition of property was required for the construction of the railway facilities in the area except on the site of King's Cross station, as immediately north of King's Cross the Great Northern Railway ran through open country.

The Locomotive Depot was built on part of a large area of land which was bounded by the embankment of the East and West India Docks and Birmingham Junction Railway to the north, the main line of the Great Northern Railway to the east, and the Regent's Canal to the south. The East and West India Docks and Birmingham Junction Railway was under construction in 1850-51 from Chalk Farm to Poplar and became known as the North London Railway in 1853.

The many activities of King's Cross Goods Yard eventually occupied all the remaining area of this land and the depot was soon surrounded by railway facilities. However, until the construction of the Midland Railway into St. Pancras in 1868 the western perimeter of the depot was terraced housing rejoicing under such names as Durham Terrace, Oxford Street, Cambridge Street, Winchester Street and Salisbury Crescent. This part of Agar Town and St. Pancras was entirely swept away by the construction of the Midland Railway, which then ran immediately alongside the back of King's Cross Depot. Although it was

Above right: GNR Locomotive Shops, London—an early plan of the depot drawn at Boston, possibly in Febuary 1849. The depot was considerably enlarged before completion in 1850. (Redrawn from an original in the Public Records Office, Porchester Road)

Below right: The Locomotive Hall, an impressive view of the interior of the depot in the early 1850s. A Bury type four-coupled engine stands in the foreground, probably one of the six built by Fairbairn in 1848-9. (Local History Collection, London Borough of Camden)

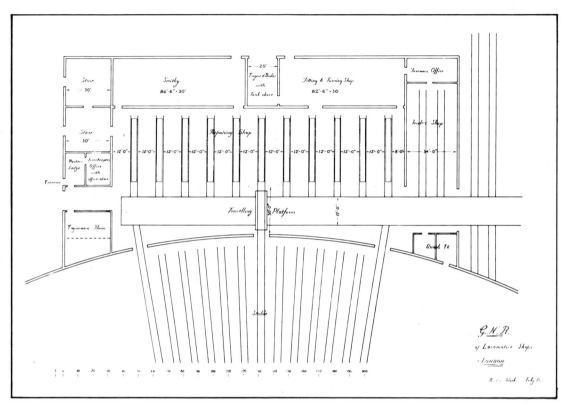

Store
30'

Smithy
86'·6"×30'

Engine & Boiler
with
Tank above
20'

Fitting & Turning Shop
82'·6"×30'

Foreman Office

Tender Shop

Store
30'

Repairing Shop

Porters
Lodge

Timekeepers
Office
with
office above

Entrance

12'·0" 12'·0" 12'·0" 12'·0" 12'·0" 12'·0" 12'·0" 12'·0" 12'·0" 12'·0" 12'·0" 8'·0" 34'·0"

Travelling Platform
11'·0"

Engineman Room

Urinals &c

Stable

G. N. R.
of Locomotive Shops
London

surrounded by railway lines one could get no sight of the depot's activities from either the Great Northern or Midland main lines, but an excellent high level view could be had from a North London Railway train travelling from Broad Street to Richmond or Watford soon after passing over the bridge high above the Great Northern Railway at Belle Isle.

In the Public Records Office at Porchester Road a plan is preserved of the original London Locomotive Shops, part of a collection of drawings prepared at Boston by Edward Bury. This was probably completed in February 1849, but the actual year is now missing from the drawing, which has been redrawn for illustration here. Edward Bury, the Locomotive Superintendent, must have had second thoughts concerning the adequacy of the facilities proposed in London, as the Board of Directors authorised the construction of the engine stables early in 1850 to an amended drawing. Bury did not remain in office whilst the depot was being built, as he resigned shortly after authorisation, and Archibald Sturrock replaced him in May 1850.

An illustration of the original depot has survived and is reproduced. This shows a considerable increase in the accommodation of the depot from the 13 roads originally envisaged to 25; each road conveniently provided with individual entrances, instead of only the three openings shown on the original drawing. The early drawing also showed a travelling platform 17 ft. long running on straight tracks immediately inside the building, which would have necessitated the uncoupling of locomotives from their tenders before they were placed on the shed roads, but it is doubtful if an engine could have used the two outer entrances to the shed as the tracks radiating fanwise outside the building were not in strict alignment with the straight travelling platform. A separate two-road tender shop was to have been provided with an additional entrance on the north side of the shed. The repair shop itself was to have contained only eleven pit roads, but there was ample blacksmith's accommodation.

One concludes that the original depot as proposed was not a running shed but was intended for engine repairs. No coking or servicing facilities were shown, but the area outside the front of the shed was marked for stabling locomotives, and much of the normal work of a depot would have had to be done in the open.

The depot as actually built in 1850 provided room for many more locomotives under cover; the travelling platform which would have taken up much accommodation in the repair shop was eliminated, and there was room for a locomotive to be serviced on each of the 25 roads without sacrifice of the eleven-road repair shop in the middle section at the back. The front of the shed building was in the shape of a shallow curve, and as the tracks did not radiate from a turntable, this gave the engine stables a unique appearance. The turntable was sited near the temporary terminal a little to the south of the arches, which eventually carried Maiden Lane over the railway.

Turntables had not been provided at many places when the

Above: The original Locomotive Shed at King's Cross with its tall chimney. Much of this original building survived until the end of steam traction in 1963. The horses in the foreground were also a Loco responsibility for shoeing. *(British Railways)*

Above right: The approximate site of the GN Locomotive Depot. The depot was eventually surrounded by railway installations on all sides.

Right: Plan of the depot in 1871. *(From an Ordnance Survey)*

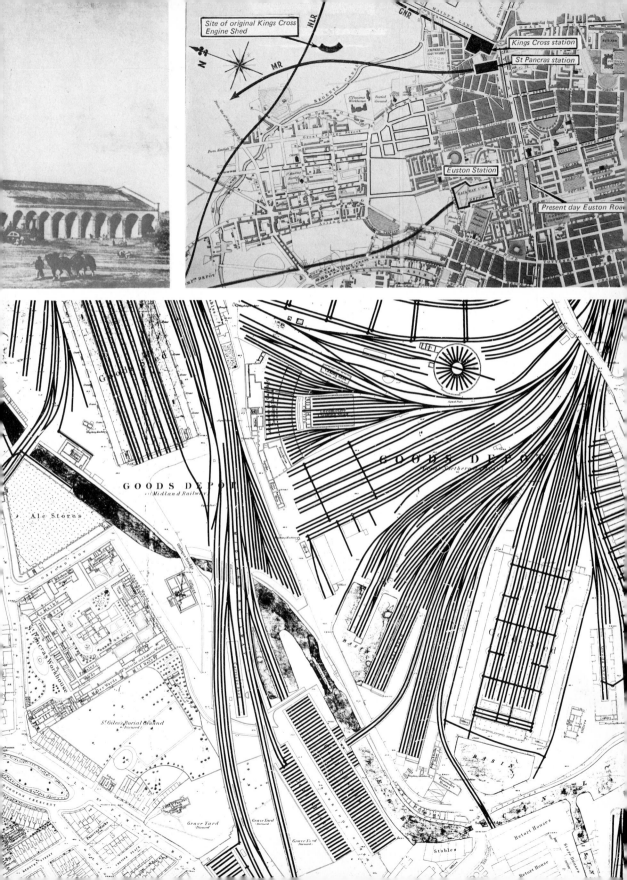

Site of original Kings Cross
Engine Shed

N

MR

NLR

GNR

Kings Cross station

St Pancras station

Euston Station

Present day Euston Road

GOODS DEPOT
of Midland Railway

GOODS DEPOT
of the Northern

Ale Stores

St Pancras Workhouse

St Giles Burial Ground
Disused

Grave Yard
Disused

Grave Yard
Disused

Grave Yard
Disused

Stables

Retort House

Retort House

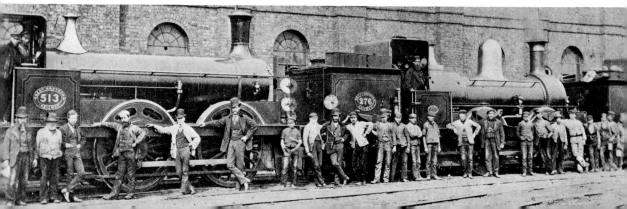

various GN lines were opened, and considerable tender-first working was required in consequence, particularly in country areas. In 1851 Sturrock requested that a number of turntables should be laid down in order to prevent accidents, but many of these were only 16 ft. in diameter and would require separation of the engine and tender for turning. The turntable provided at the London depot was, however, 40 ft. in diameter. It was also decided in that year to fit lifeguards generally on tenders.

Most of the various sidings and facilities, which eventually were constructed in the King's Cross Goods Yard, were spread out fanwise from a common throat in the Belle Isle area. This was possibly the reason for the fan-shaped spread of tracks and the curved shed front of the locomotive depot.

A large part of the original 1850 building remained in use for engine repairs until the depot was closed in 1963, although many other changes had been made to the depot during the intervening years. Messrs. Easton & Amos of Southwark were responsible for the steam engine pumps and blowing apparatus installed in the shops soon after construction. Four cranes and a traveller were also ordered in 1850 and it appears that the shops were well equipped for lifting locomotives, or their component parts. During the next decade only minor alterations and additions were made, the most expensive item being the additional coke sidings for engines put down in 1856 at a cost of £1,063. Coke was then the standard fuel used in steam engines, although trials had already commenced with coal, which was considerably cheaper, and within a few years was being used increasingly, particularly on goods engines.

In order to light the fires in engines a furnace had been designed in August 1850 to prepare the coke, which probably used the coke dropped from fires on arrival on the shed.

In January 1852 the Locomotive Superintendent thought it would be prudent to have a second pump and boiler put down in case of casualty to the one provided when the depot had been built. These steam-driven pumps would be used for pumping the locomotive water supply, which came from the nearby Regent's Canal, into the overhead storage tank. Although the Great Northern Railway was paying £350 per annum in 1850 to the Regent's Canal Company for the supply of water for the station at Maiden Lane, five years later the Engineer questioned with the Great Northern Railway Board the rather slender arrangement with the Canal Company, but the Board resolved not to disturb it.

The first breakdown crane for London was delivered in 1855 by Messrs. Bray and Waddington of Leeds at a cost of £150, but it would have been of little practical value at it was hand-operated and of very limited lifting capacity.

In 1857 a number of machines were ordered for the machine shop adjacent to the Repair Shop including a bolt and nut screwing machine, a portable punch and shearing machine, and a hand punching press and a lathe, which it was decided should be made in the Doncaster Works.

A new turntable of 40 ft. diameter was ordered at a cost of £500 in 1855, as the site of the old one was required in order to allow the development of the Potato Market and the approach lines into the Goods Yard. Sturrock had already requested the provision of a second turntable; he pointed out that if the present turntable were to fail there would be no means of turning engines and he was much opposed to tender-first working on express passenger trains. Several sites were considered in the area where it was eventually placed in latter years, but there was difficulty in deciding where to put it and finally it was recommended that it should be sited as far as possible from the goods yard lines in order to leave room for additional tracks. The turntable was put down much nearer to the Engine Stables on the north side of the Loco. Yard, but it was not long before further developments required the turntable to be moved again. A map of King's Cross Goods Yard of about 1860 clearly shows that there was a triangle of lines in the yard, but whether this was used for the turning of engines is not known.

Difficulty was experienced with the carriage repair shop, which had been authorised in November 1851, to be built between the coke shed and the engine stables, as the Locomotive Foreman, Mr. Budge, received notice nine months later to quit the land on which it had been built. The land had been sold to someone who required to build houses on it. Although a short-term agreement was sought for three years, and after one year it was hoped to transfer the carriage repair work to Doncaster, it was decided in January 1853 to build a replacement for the carriage repair depot in the King's Cross Station below the canal at a cost of £975. A small donkey engine with boiler and shafting to drive a drill and circular saw were authorised in 1855 for this facility.

The question of building houses had been raised very soon after the depot had been built, in the form of a petition from 37 of the locomotive workmen employed there who complained of high house rents. This had been supported by their Foreman with a suggestion that the company should build houses for the men on the spare ground behind the engine house. The Board of Directors resolved that this was not advisable and suggested if any party would build on any spare ground belonging to the company it would be favourably considered. Nothing appears to have come of this suggestion, as a further memorial was received from the staff in 1853. It was not until 1892 that the block of flats known as Culross Buildings were built in Battlebridge Road as a replacement for dwellings which had been demolished to make way for extensions on the suburban side of the station and to house some of the many railway employees in the King's Cross area.

In September 1860 the General Manager asked for an engine turntable to be put down at King's Cross Station. Although this was sanctioned by the Great Northern Railway Board, a few weeks later it was decided that it would be of little use without the provision of an engine shed and other facilities. Two plans were considered for building a depot at the station. One depended

Below: Stirling 7 ft. 6 in. single No. 872 in 1901, after being overhauled, a new boiler fitted and repainted in the Front Erecting Shop. This was the last engine to be fully overhauled at King's Cross. *(K. H. Leech collection)*

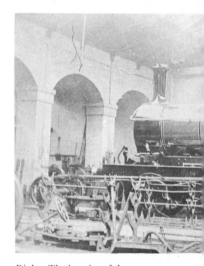

Right: The interior of the back erecting shop where a suburban tank, LNER Class C12, is being retubed, and the pistons examined on an Atlantic. *(K. H. Leech collection)*

Far right: The Front Erecting Shop in 1927. The floor is covered with wooden headstocks from wagons. *(British Railways/Fox Photos)*

Right: The main line
running shed early in the
twentieth century. The
photograph was most
probably taken on a Sunday
morning as the yard is full
almost to capacity.
(R. A. H. Weight collection)

Centre right: Stirling 8 ft. 0 in.
single on the 40 ft. 0 in.
turntable at Top Shed
before it was replaced in
1901 by a larger turntable
capable of turning the
Atlantics. Turntables
occupied at least five
different sites at Top Shed
during the depot's existence.
(I. Allan collection)

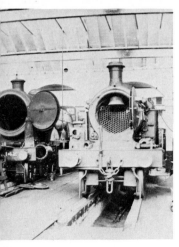

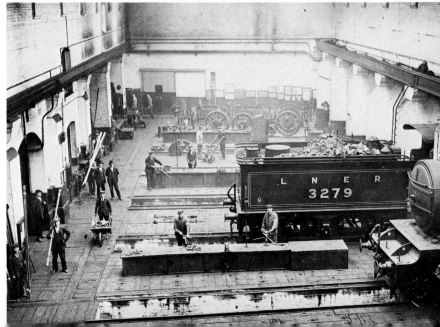

upon obtaining the houses on the Drakefield Estate adjoining the station. The alternative scheme, however, which was the one adopted, involved the conversion of the small carriage repair shop which had been built at King's Cross Station in 1853 into an engine shed for six locomotives and the provision of alternative facilities for carriage repairs. The building of a turntable and small locomotive depot at King's Cross Station must have been very welcome, as until these facilities were constructed early in 1862 all engines had to use the single track of the down main line, pass through the tunnel under the Regent's Canal and proceed to the locomotive depot in King's Cross Goods Yard.

In order to replace the small carriage repair shop at the station, a part of the original engine stables in King's Cross Goods Yard was converted and extended for the purpose. By 1861 the original engine stables were also becoming inadequate for the increased number of locomotives allocated and working into London, and in October of that year tenders had been called for the construction of an additional new engine shed, additions to the repair shops, and the above-mentioned alterations to part of the existing building for carriage repairs.

The contract was given to Messrs. Kirk & Parry Ltd. and in February 1862 it was reported that the contractors were pushing ahead with the work, which was completed by the end of the year. The total cost of providing these additional engine facilities at the station and the goods yard was over £25,000 and some £3,000 more than estimated.

The provision of these additional facilities, especially at the station, were of particular value in 1862 as there was a considerable increase in special trains to London for the International Exhibition held in that year. The building of this engine shed at the north end of the departure platform at King's Cross station was no doubt the reason for the name "TOP SHED" that was commonly applied to the locomotive premises at the slightly higher level of King's Cross Goods Yard, although this name does not appear to have received any official recognition until mentioned in a Board Minute of 1909.

The completely new engine shed in the Goods Yard was built immediately in front of the original engine stables and consisted of eight straight and parallel roads, only one of which was projected through the back of the shed and provided access to the Repair Shop in the original building by means of a traverser that served eight of the shop roads. This eight-road shed was, in its early days, known as the Locomotive Cleaning Shed and would be used for servicing locomotives. It was later known as the Main Line Running Shed and remained in use until 1963.

Additional machinery was authorised for the King's Cross Locomotive Works, which was the title of the repairing establishment about this time. A steam hammer was authorised in 1862, several machines, including a 15 in. lathe, a shaping machine with three heads and a drilling machine, in 1863, and in 1864 Sturrock requested that as the stationary engine power was rather

Above: The Blacksmiths' Shop, King's Cross, had been provided with ample blacksmiths' accommodation from the time of the depot's construction in 1850. A hundred years later only one or two fires remained in use. *(British Railways/Fox Photos)*

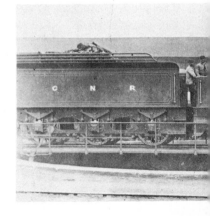

deficient, a stationary engine recently acquired by the company should be converted and installed at King's Cross to drive the machinery. This was a beam engine and it is believed that it was obtained locally in Agar Town at a cost of about £500. Already about 50 years old when purchased, this old beam engine was used at Top Shed to drive practically all the machinery in the machine shop. It gave excellent service, requiring little maintenance and giving no trouble over its total working life of approximately 120 years. In 1929 it was still in use, but shortly afterwards it was carefully dismantled and later re-assembled in York Railway Museum, where it was displayed until the museum closed at the end of 1973.

King's Cross for many years carried out heavy repairs and overhauled locomotives completely, including lifting boilers out of the frames and repainting. Patrick Stirling had made a tour of the out-station depots soon after his appointment to the Great Northern Railway in 1866 and although he expressed surprise at the extent of the repairs carried out—as he remarked, "not too economically either"—the practice continued at Top Shed for many more years. A photograph has survived of the last locomotive overhauled at King's Cross repair works. It was a single, No. 872, which was finished in 1901. In addition to being completely overhauled, the locomotive received a new cab, springs and boiler; it was completely repainted and distinctively the lining out was also applied round the dome.

In 1902 a number of staff were evidently discharged at the London Locomotive Works due to the recent introduction of mechanical appliances at Doncaster Works, which were considerably extended at this time, and the Directors made available a grant of £300 for compensation in special cases. The main repair shop, however, continued to be used for the more usual types of depot repairs to locomotives until the final closure of the depot.

A drawing of the depot, dated 1890, shows that of the original 25 roads in the engine stables, the middle eleven tracks were still used for the repair of locomotives as they had been since the depot was built. The front of this building had a lower roof and was called the Back Erecting Shop. The same eleven roads were continued into a much larger and higher building called the Front Erecting Shop, and leading from this were the blacksmiths' forges, and nearby the turnery, machine shops, carpenters' shop and the coppersmiths' shop.

The Front Erecting Shop was served by an overhead travelling crane of 20 tons capacity and it was here that locomotives were overhauled. The seven shorter roads at the south end were shown as the Paint and Carpenters' Shop and the other seven roads at the north end, which had been extended in length in 1862 and made into the Carriage & Wagon Repair Shop, were divided into two sections retaining the front part of the original engine shed as the Back Carriage Shop, and the extension at the rear was the Front Carriage Shop.

Below: Stirling four-coupled passenger engine No. 201, built in 1882, on the 40 ft. 0 in. turntable at Top Shed. *(K. H. Leech collection)*

2

The Midland Roundhouse

In December 1857 the Midland Railway reached agreement with the Great Northern Railway for running powers over the Great Northern main line from Hitchin to King's Cross. Under the Heads of Agreement for a Traffic Arrangement the Great Northern Railway agreed *inter alia* to provide at their own cost engine sheds for occupation by the Midland Railway. The Midland was to pay for the water provided for their engines at the cost price, and 6 per cent. interest per annum on the cost of providing the locomotive premises was to be paid annually for their rent and dilapidation. In December 1857 the Great Northern Railway Board of Directors approved an estimate for the engine shed, sidings, the removal of the turntable and earthworks of £10,482, the Midland Railway expressing their satisfaction but subject to the approval of their Locomotive Superintendent, Matthew Kirtley, who had been instructed to meet Sturrock and arrange for the accommodation of the Midland locomotives at King's Cross.

In February 1858 the Midland Railway commenced through running of their passenger trains into King's Cross Station and of their goods trains some eight months later. In August the Midland opened their own booking office at King's Cross, but in the same month the Engineer of the Great Northern Railway reported that, whilst the buildings for the Midland Railway's goods business were nearly completed, the area for the engine shed had only just been cleared and that the latter's foundations were built only to ground level. In the event the engine shed, which was a round house, was not completed until February 1859, one year after Midland Railway services had commenced to run into King's Cross. It was built on a site immediately adjacent to the Great Northern Railway locomotive depot yard, a little to the east and north of the original Great Northern Railway engine stable buildings, and was provided with its own coking and watering facilities.

The site of the Top Shed Locomotive Sheds has been in recent years almost entirely level, but it is apparent from contemporary records that considerable exacavation of the site had to be carried

Top: Midland Railway Kirtley single No. 28 allocated to the Midland Depot at King's Cross. This was one of four locomotives of this class working from the depot in 1864. *(British Railways)*

Centre left: After a period of use for carriage repairs the Midland Railway Roundhouse became the stable of many of the King's Cross suburban tank engines. Three Sturrock front-coupled suburban tanks of 1865-6 sit round the turntable in this photograph with a similar Stirling engine of 1870. *(K. H. Leech collection)*

Centre right: A later interior view of the roundhouse with an Ivatt ten-wheeled tank and Stirling tender engine occupying the stalls. *(B. Deer)*

Bottom: Five Gresley N2s in the roundhouse in the early 1920's. *(M. Elvey)*

18

out to make room for the construction of the Midland roundhouse, as over 27,000 cu. yds. of spoil were removed and transported to Holloway and Hornsey. In September 1860 an earth slip occurred, which had to be removed; the Great Northern Railway Board decided to charge the money involved to capital and 6 per cent. per annum was to be paid by the Midland Railway. Up to the end of 1860 the Midland Railway had still not paid any rent for the use of the engine shed, as they considered the charge for earthworks was in excess of what had been required for the needs of the Midland Railway, but this was resolved the following year.

The roundhouse was of substantial size and eventually 24 roads radiated from the 40-ft. diameter turntable installed. Originally four engine pits were provided and it is likely that until 1862 only 16 tracks were actually laid down inside the shed. The Midland Railway decided in 1861 to build their own Goods and Mineral Station at Agar Town and vacate the Great Northern Railway King's Cross Goods Yard premises. The Great Northern Railway agreed to lay a double line to their boundary and the Midland agreed to continue paying rent for the engine house. A month later, in connection with their new Goods Station, the Midland Railway made application for an additional length of rails at the east end of their engine shed. This was agreed by the Great Northern Railway subject to removal if the Great Northern Company required it. In July 1862 the Midland Railway vacated the goods yard premises at King's Cross but, whilst the Midland complained bitterly of being evicted overnight by the Great Northern Railway from the Great Northern Goods Yard, the roundhouse continued to be used by the Midland Railway.

In December 1862 the Midland requested the construction of seven additional pits in the engine shed used at King's Cross and the Great Northern Railway agreed to pay the £637 cost involved provided that the Midland Railway again agreed to pay annually 6 per cent. on the outlay. In 1863 the Midland requested an alteration to the roof of the coke stage at a cost of £50 and it was resolved by the Great Northern Railway Directors at the expense of the Midland Railway. About this time a long single siding was provided for coking Midland locomotives at King's Cross Station so as to avoid the occupation of the track in sending locomotives to the roundhouse in the goods yard.

In February 1863 the Midland gave notice to terminate the seven years' Traffic Agreement, but the Midland Railway ceased to use the Great Northern Railway line into King's Cross after October 1 1868, when their own lines into St. Pancras were brought into use but before the notice had expired. Some Midland goods trains had commenced to run from Bedford to St. Pancras in September 1867, but Midland passenger trains ran into King's Cross until the end of September 1868 and it is most probable that the roundhouse was vacated about this time. The General Manager of the Great Northern Railway, Mr. Seymour Clarke, was advised on October 20 1868 that Mr. Jackson, the Midland

Top left: The exterior of the roundhouse in 1904. The water tank provided for Midland Railway locomotives is on the left and the central lantern of the roundhouse is still in position. Later the section of the roof over the turntable was removed. (P. N. Townend collection)

Top right: The roundhouse being dismantled in 1931. The new coaling plant is under construction on the left of the photograph. The young man in the foreground, later Chief Clerk at the depot, produced this photograph from his wallet over 40 years later, some years after he had retired. (A. R. Smith)

Centre: Rail motor No. 2, used on the Edgware branch, with the roundhouse in the background. (E. Pouteau)

Bottom: The site of the roundhouse after demolition. The tracks were used for a period for stabling locomotives and subsequently the Back Pits were laid out on the site. (H. Kelson)

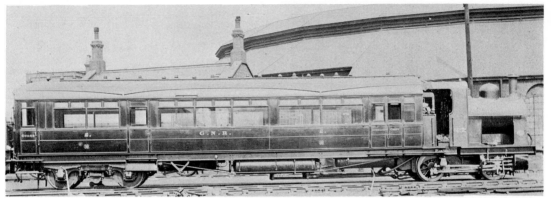

Locomotive Superintendent, still held the keys of the engine shed and it was not until early November that the keys were received by the Great Northern Railway; they were accepted without prejudice to the legal aspects of non-expiry of the required seven years notice. By this time the total cost of the engine shed had risen to £21,380.13s.10d. and the outstanding rent for the period of 18 months remaining amounted to £1,924.5s.3d. In September 1869 the Midland Railway agreed to pay a total of £24,000 as a discharge of their liability in respect of the Traffic Agreement for the use of the G.N. line between Hitchin and King's Cross, which no doubt included the debt for the locomotive shed rent. In 1870 the Great Northern Railway received an application from the Regent Canal Company for payment of the water used by Midland Railway locomotives from 1860-67, and itself settled the bill for £816.13s.4d.

Despite extensive enquiries it has not been possible to find any illustration of the round shed when in use by the Midland Railway. An old roster for regularly manned Midland locomotives, however, has survived from 1864 and shows that four Kirtley double-framed 2-2-2s (Nos. 26, 28, 30, 39), newly built at Derby Works, were working from King's Cross at that time, together with eight double-framed 0-6-0 Kirtley standard goods engines (Nos. 481, 483, 484, 485, 487, 488, 489, 490) built by Robert Stephenson & Co. in 1863. One of the King's Cross 2-2-2s, No. 30, survived until 1904-5 and was the last Midland Railway 2-2-2 in service. These singles were replaced in 1867 on the King's Cross to Leicester services by some new Kirtley-designed 2-4-0s built by Beyer Peacock, mainly in the series 180 to 189. Locomotives of this class also survived into the early years of this century, but the Kirtley 0-6-0s were members of a large class which were exceptionally long-lived; the last of them were not withdrawn until 1951 under British Railways ownership.

The Great Northern Railway put their only roundhouse to good use after it was vacated by the Midland Railway, initially for accommodating carriage and wagon repairs, but within a few years to provide much-needed extra accommodation for their own locomotives. Until it was finally demolished it was still known as The Derby Shed, although built and paid for by the Great Northern Railway. The turntable remained 40 ft. in diameter, but eventually out of the 24 roads radiating from it 22 were given pits. There was a separate coaling stage, water tank and offices for the Derby Shed. Towards the end of its life the centre portion of the roof of the shed had been open to atmosphere, but previously, for many years, this had been roofed and fitted with suitable openings for venting smoke and a high lantern in the centre.

In earlier years Great Northern Railway tender locomotives could use the round shed, but by 1931 few tender engines were left at King's Cross short enough to be accommodated on the 40 ft. diameter turntable; during the 1920s the building had been principally used by tank engines, mainly N2s, which invariably worked out of King's Cross chimney first and therefore rarely required turning in any case. The depot at Top Shed had long been entirely hemmed in by the King's Cross Goods Yard and the only way better facilities could be provided and the layout improved was by the demoliton of the Derby roundhouse. In 1931 this was carried out on a "do-it-yourself" basis by two steam locomotives. The turntable was suitably protected by sleepers. An N1 was then hitched onto the shed in one direction and a J52 fastened to the shed at an angle of 45 deg. to the N1. Both locomotives were given steam and the shed came down in an enormous cloud of black dust. The turntable and radiating roads were in open-air use for a short time until eventually the "back pits" were built on the site.

By the time of its demolition the Derby roundhouse had received many battle scars from engines going through the outside wall on the different roads. Great Northern locomotives would appear to have been singularly unsuitable for stabling in a round house. Latterly they had been fitted with vacuum brakes, which would not be operative when the engine was low in steam, and a horizontal pull-out regulator handle which should have been secured in the closed position by a thumbscrew on its quadrant in the cab, but which, if this was not done, had a tendency to spring open. Upon being lit up from cold, despite the various instructions about fastening the regulator handle, opening the cylinder cocks, putting the reverser in mid-gear, fully applying the hand brake, and so on, a locomotive would occasionally set off on its own when sufficient steam had been generated to move it, with consequent damage to anything in the way. Moving locomotives into the roundhouse also tended to be hazardous, as frequently only the hand brake could be used. A locomotive which had no steam up at all had to be pulled around the yard in reverse by another until enough compression had been created in the boiler for it to move off the turntable under its own power.

Bill Harvey, for many years Shed Master at Norwich and who was at King's Cross in the late 1920s, related to me that he had some work to carry out on a J52 saddle tank in the roundhouse which required the locomotive setting in a different position. He asked the Assistant Superintendent for this to be done and that gentleman, helped by another young man who later became the Motive Power Officer of the Eastern Region, decided to do the job on their own rather than detailing a driver and fireman. The J52 would not move in the right direction, so the reversing lever was pulled over. The locomotive thereupon shot through the wall of the shed, making two round holes in the brickwork with its buffers. When they got it forward they nearly put the locomotive into the turntable pit. Once more it was reversed and the next thing the acting crew remembered was the sight of a considerable amount of daylight where there should have been none and the engine's bunker full of bricks. Setting Great Northern locomotives was evidently a tricky business, but in 1931 the Derby Round Shed and the last traces of the separate Midland Railway Depot finally disappeared.

3

Developments at
the London Depot

After the Midland Railway had vacated the roundhouse in 1868 the Great Northern had the use of three separate sheds, all within a few yards of each other, collectively known as "Top Shed". They remained in use with only minor alterations for the next 60 years. The entrance line to the depot must have been difficult to operate in conditions of adverse visibility, as it was also used by engines departing from the shed. It was not until 1878 that the Directors authorised £1,600 to make a double line for engines working between the locomotive shed and the outlet of King's Cross goods yard at the delightfully named "Pigeon House" signalbox. This work was completed in April 1879, but the signals controlling the outlet to the depot were eventually transferred to Goods & Mineral Junction signalbox — probably in 1899, when further alterations to the engine lines were made and two signalboxes altered in order to improve the working of the goods yard. Goods & Mineral Junction signalbox was still in use in 1975.

About 1884 Top Shed acquired an unusual item in the form of a bell from an American locomotive. This bell had been fitted to a locomotive called *Lovett Eames,* which was the 5,000th locomotive built by Baldwin & Co. in 1880. The locomotive was a 4-2-2 tender locomotive with 6 ft. 6 in. diameter driving wheels, a Wootten firebox with a huge 56 sq.ft. grate area, and it weighed 38 tons in working order. It had been built for express passenger service on the Philadelphia & Reading Railroad but, despite some fast runs, was apparently unsuccessful. Mr. Lovett Eames, an American inventor, purchased the locomotive in order to demonstrate the efficiency of a vacuum brake he had invented, and shipped it over to England in 1881. *Lovett Eames* was erected at the Miles Platting Works of the Lancashire & Yorkshire Railway early in 1882, and in July of that year was exhibited at Alexandra Palace amongst a collection of life-saving appliances, Mr. Eames apparently considered that his vacuum brake came within that category. It was intended that the locomotive should run as a working demonstration of the Eames duplex automatic vacuum brake, and in March 1882 Eames applied to the Great

Above: *Lovett Eames,* the 5000th locomotive built by Baldwins. The bell from this engine was used for many years at King's Cross and Hornsey Locomotive Depots to ring the time for the repair staff. A portrait of Mr. Lovett Eames is displayed on the cab side. *(Baldwin Loco Works)*

Below: Stirling suburban tank No. 119, built 1871, near the roundhouse which was the home of many of the suburban locomotives for over fifty years. *(I. Allan collection)*

Above: The ashpit area and coaling platform, with the Midland Railway Roundhouse in the background. *(I. Allan collection)*

Below: The main-line running shed showing the hydraulic lift on the right-hand side of the photograph. No shelter was provided at this time for staff engaged on lifting locomotives. The earlier hand operated hoist on the front of the shed spanned two roads. *(I. Allan collection)*

Bottom right: No. 1636, a Gresley mixed-traffic small-boilered 2-6-0 (LNER Class K1) alongside the rear of the coaling stage building. *(Real Photographs)*

Right: Stirling single
No. 547 being lifted on the
hoist outside the Running
Shed. A considerable height
was required in order to
clear the 8 ft. 0 in. driving
wheels. *(K. H. Leech
collection)*

Below: In the background to
this photograph of Stirling
front four-coupled engine
No. 10A can be seen the
smoke chutes added to the
roof of the Loco and
Carriage Repair Shops. The
tall chimney on the left was
fitted to one of the
locomotive-type stationary
boilers provided for the hot
water washing-out of
boilers. *(P. N. Townend
collection)*

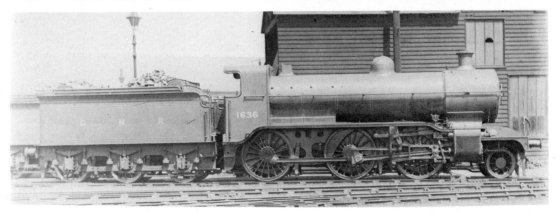

Northern Railway Board for permission to run his engine on the Great Northern line. Mr. Patrick Stirling was asked by the Directors to assess the locomotive. Two months later he reported back that he could not recommend it to run on any trains on the Great Northern Railway. The offer to fit a train with the Eames brake was also turned down. Stirling stated that he did not consider there were sufficient advantages over the present brake to induce the company to complicate the working by the addition of another brake system. He further warned the Board to be extremely careful to avoid anything that might be construed as recognition of the system.

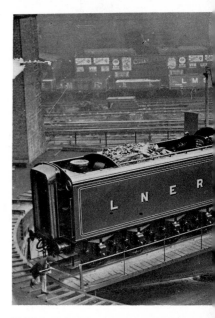

After the exhibition at Alexandra Palace the locomotive was stabled in an old GNR shed at Wood Green, from whence it has been said that it made sporadic trips to demonstrate the brake. In view of Patrick Stirling's expressed views to the GNR Board this would appear to be extremely doubtful, at least so far as the Great Northern was concerned. Thus the opportunity to gain experience with a wide firebox single-wheeler was lost!

In May 1884 the Great Northern Railway Board's solicitor reported that the locomotive, which had been left with the Company by Mr. Eames, had been sold by auction for £165. Mr. Eames had asked the Company to find standing room for the locomotive for about six weeks in June whilst he returned to America. He was, however, assassinated in July 1882 and the locomotive had been left in the hands of the Great Northern Railway. The Great Northern claimed the sum of £61.12s.10d. for expenses and so, after deducting the auctioneer's charges, the balance of £74.4s.0d. was paid into court for the legal representatives of Mr. Eames—a scarcely princely sum for a locomotive only four years old! The scrap merchant who had purchased the engine in April 1884 cut it up on site at Wood Green, but the bell found its way to King's Cross Shed. About 1909 the bell was transferred to the locomotive shed which had been built at Hornsey ten years previously and until 1938 it was used as a time signal for fitting staff who worked there.

At a little ceremony in July 1938 the bell, which had been suitably mounted and engraved by Sir Nigel Gresley, was presented by Sir Ralph Wedgewood, Chief General Manager, on behalf of the London & North Eastern Railway to a Mr. Richard E. Pennoyer who was attached to the American Embassy in London. He is said to have long wished to have a locomotive bell and would provide a good home for it. Guests at his home were "gonged" for dinner on the bell, but at Top Shed the men were called after 1909 by a steam-operated buzzer. A large framed photograph of *Lovett Eames* hung in the offices for many years afterwards.

In 1882 the Great Northern Railway Board Directors visited the King's Cross Goods Yard to decide on the desirability of removing the engine sheds to Harringay and converting the Top Shed site into a yard for goods traffic. The whole depot was hemmed in by the goods yard facilities, which were themselves incapable of

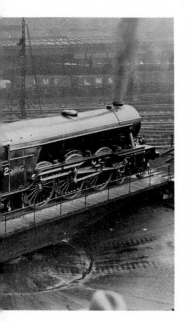

Above: Stirling 8 ft. 0 in. single No. 2 is standing in the King's Cross Station Loco Yard. In the background can be seen a little of the three-road Loco Shed constructed in 1876. This shed was demolished about 1893 together with the wall behind the locomotive, in order to enlarge the suburban station. (K. H. Leech collection)

Above left: No. 4472 being pushed round on the 70 ft. diameter turntable installed at King's Cross Station by the tunnel mouth in 1928. A corridor tender is fitted for the non-stop working to Edinburgh introduced in that year. (Daily Mirror)

Left: King's Cross Station Loco. Depot yard in 1953. The depot was moved to this position in 1923, involving considerable excavation and removal of a barge dock off the Regent's Canal which served the Imperial Gas Works. Two bridges also once spanned the railway tracks on this site. (A. H. Gosford/British Railways)

further expansion, as the Great Northern had by then purchased and occupied the whole of the land bounded by the Midland Railway on the west, the North London Railway on the north, the Great Northern lines on the east, and the Regent's Canal to the south and west.

Although pressure must have been great to move the locomotive establishment and plans were prepared for doing so, nothing came of the proposals immediately. In 1892 Patrick Stirling, however, requested the Board to approve the construction of a number of new locomotive depots throughout the line and amongst these was included a proposal for a depot for 50 engines with repair shops, turntable and sidings at Ferme Park at an estimated cost of £50,000. In 1894 priority was given for the construction of depots at Grantham and Colwick, but although the construction of a depot had not been authorised work was already proceeding to prepare the site at Ferme Park, as over £12,000 was spent on such work in that year.

The justification for the provision of engine sheds at Ferme Park was stated to be the need of prompt recoaling and watering of engines in order to reduce the working time of heavy trains between Peterborough and London. In 1898 the principle of building an engine shed on the up side of the main line at Ferme Park to accommodate 40 large engines and tenders, so as to relieve the shed at King's Cross, was formally approved. The firm of Kirk Knight & Co. of Sleaford was given the contract at £32,499 and the work was to be completed by July 1 1899 with the proviso that

The main-line running shed and coaling platform in 1931 from the top of the new coaling plant, then under construction. The old coaling platform was constructed in wood originally, but later renewed in brick. *(C. C. B. Herbert)*

part, including the coal stage, was to be ready by May 1 1899, or earlier if possible. The tender of Messrs. Kirk Knight & Co. was dated September 14 1898 and little time was allowed to carry out the work, which was, however, completed during the summer of 1899. The tremendous increase about this time in freight traffic must have placed an intolerable burden both on the facilities at Top Shed and on the lines that gave access to the depot. In 1900 further work was authorised at Horsey Depot, including creation of a site to stack coal and the provision of a set of sheer legs for lifting engines.

In May 1901 a further considerable sum of £15,938 was authorised to provide a new coal stage in the Loco. Yard at Top Shed, as well as to carry out certain alterations and additions to the lines adjacent to the stage and engine shed. The engine turntable was once more moved, this time from a site near the front of the main line shed to the end of the spur near the loco. residence. The new coal stage was built close to where the turntable had been sited for many years and a number of additional sidings were laid nearby to obtain a much-needed increase in standing space for locomotives. Work on a new 52 ft. turntable had been allowed to precede the other alterations, and a Mr. Wall was permitted to commence construction of the foundations in January 1900, on the unusual terms of cost plus 10 per cent., but the job was not completed for some six months. The construction of the new Ivatt Atlantic locomotives in 1898 and from 1900 had made it urgently necessary to provide longer

Plan of the depot as altered in the reconstruction of 1931-3. *(British Railways)*

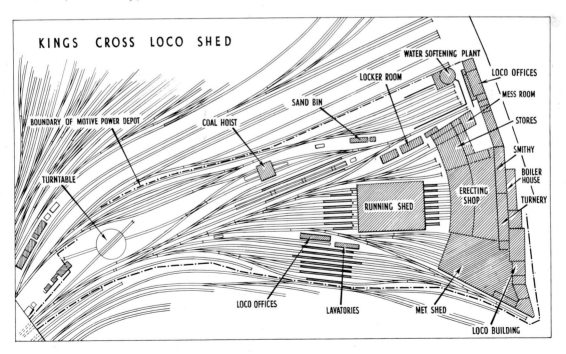

Above: 30-ton electrically operated Royce crane installed in the erecting shop in 1931, lifting an N2. A caption at the time stated the crane was the latest in engineering, installed in the engine hospital at King's Cross *(Express Photos/ British Railways)*

Right: Class N2 No. 4747 being spray-cleaned with hot water in the Met. Shed in 1933. *(Graphic Photo/ British Railways)*

turntables; each time one of these locomotives worked into King's Cross it had to be sent to Ferme Park to be turned on a triangle, a return journey of over eight miles.

The largest turntable in the London area at that time was one of a nominal 50 ft. diameter at Holloway Carriage Sidings. This had been put down in 1893 and two engine pits had also been provided. The new carriage sidings were brought into use at that point in the following year. These engine facilities at Holloway were provided for train engines working empty coaches out of King's Cross and in order to reduce the number of engines going to Top Shed for servicing requirements. A turntable of 50 ft. diameter would have been a little too tight to turn an Atlantic, which had an overall wheelbase of 48 ft. 5¾ in., as the turntable at Holloway was later recorded as being only 49 ft. 7 in. long.

Construction of the new coaling stage at Top Shed in 1901 was followed by the provision of two stationary steam cranes for the lifting of coal tubs on to the engine tenders and bunkers. A few years later the coaling stage was extended and a further steam crane provided; these steam cranes were made at Doncaster Works and cost about £135 each. The coal stage consisted of two platforms with a coal wagon road running through the centre. Coal was shovelled out of the wagons on both sides into 10-cwt. tubs, which were then lifted with the steam cranes. The quantity of coal used at this coaling stage in 1929 was stated to be 1,530 tons per week.

The carriage repair shop roof and that of the back erecting shop were renewed at a considerable cost in 1905-06; these roofs were those over the original engine stables. About this time individual smoke chutes were added also to the erecting shop and carriage shop roofs. It would appear, therefore, that locomotives also used the carriage shop.

Additional pit accommodation was provided at Top Shed in 1909 and in 1910 a plant was authorised for washing out locomotive boilers in the Running Shed. This was supplied by the Economical Boiler Washing Company and with fittings cost £2,000. The provision of this plant considerably reduced the time required to wash out locomotive boilers. It was sited at the north-east corner of the repair shop and steam was supplied to it from a stationary boiler which stood in the open nearby. An engine with 60 lb. pressure in the boiler could be coupled to the plant, the boiler blown down, washed out, and filled with clean hot water again in many hours less than the time normally required when using cold water.

During the First World War accommodation was provided for the convenience of women cleaners employed in cleaning engines in the shed.

In October 1918 the purchase of a hydraulically-operated engine wheel drop was sanctioned. This was manufactured by Messrs. Cowan & Sheldon, but the installation was not completed until April 1921. Before this was introduced locomotives requiring only a pair of wheels to be changed were usually lifted with sheer legs; of these King's Cross had been provided with two sets, both in the open, one outside the front of the Running Shed and one near the Midland roundhouse. The latter set was hydraulically-operated and a small wooden shed was built around it at a later date. With the wheel drop hot boxes could be dealt with more easily and expeditiously. As the drop was put inside the Back Erecting Shop, working conditions in wintertime must have also been considerably improved.

With a wheel drop, the wheels are lowered into a pit underneath the locomotive, another set of rails are moved back into position, and the locomotive can then be pinched or hauled out of the way and the wheels brought up for attention. In 1938, when the Stirling 8 ft. single No. 1 was returned to service for a short time, it arrived at King's Cross with a hot driving axlebox. It was found that 8 ft. diameter wheels were too large to be dealt with on the wheel drop and the axleboxes were only with difficulty removed by lowering the wheels as far as possible and then removing the axleboxes by hand. Nevertheless, the hot box was dealt with overnight and No. 1 worked its train the next day.

The last depot alterations at King's Cross sanctioned by the Great Northern Railway were authorised late in 1922, immediately before the railway lost its identity under the Amalgamation and became part of the London & North Eastern Railway. These alterations involved considerable improvements at the north-west corner of King's Cross Station, among which the Locomotive Yard was moved to its present-day location, under dieselisation.

As mentioned earlier, the first locomotive shed at the station had been converted in 1862 from the Carriage Repair Shop and held six locomotives. A turntable and other facilities for servicing engines were installed at the same time. This depot was sited at the north end of the main departure platform and on its west side. The connecting lines to and from the King's Cross Metropolitan Railway Station were opened in 1863 and shortly afterwards a joint passenger service with the London, Chatham & Dover Railway commenced running to and from Ludgate Hill, Herne Hill and, later, Victoria. At first it was the practice for the trains arriving at King's Cross from these places to come out of the Hotel Curve Tunnel and back into King's Cross Station. Additional platform accommodation to deal with this traffic was soon provided on the hotel curve and at York Road, but more platforms were required for the increasing number of local trains starting from King's Cross Station.

In 1873 authority had been given for the duplication of the tunnels at Maiden Lane and under Copenhagen Fields, and in 1876 a new locomotive depot was constructed by Messrs. Jackson & Shaw at King's Cross Station in order that suburban platforms could be built on the site of the first locomotive shed. The new platforms were separated from the new locomotive shed and yard by a long brick wall, which supported the roof over the new platforms. The new engine shed, consisting of three roads, was

Above: The 70 ft. diameter turntable being installed at Top Shed in 1932 with the help of the breakdown crane and several members of the breakdown gang. (Fox Photos/British Railways)

Centre left: A4 No. 4903 *Peregrine* on the Top Shed turntable after it had been fitted with a vacuum tractor. The vacuum motor is coupled to the vacuum pipe on the front of the locomotive and the locomotive then turned itself. The vacuum reservoir underneath the table was of sufficient capacity to turn an engine either not in steam or not vacuum fitted. (Sport & General/British Railways)

Below left: Gresley two-cylinder Class O1 2-8-0 (later Class O3) damaged by the bomb which fell on "The Continent". (British Railways)

immediately to the west of this wall and very close to where the suburban station concourse is today. A new turntable was provided nearby, also a new tank house, workshops and coaling stage.

The new engine shed remained in use until about 1893, when the suburban station was again further expanded to the west; this once more resulted in the demolition of the small engine shed. Another higher brick wall was built in order to support the suburban station roof, which still covers No. 9-11 platforms, and provided a background for many photographs of GN locomotives taken from around the turn of the century. The turntable, coaling stage and locomotive yard remained in use for another 30 years on the reduced site between the wall and the line which emerged via the Hotel Curve Tunnel from King's Cross Metropolitan Railway Station into the present No. 14 platform.

Between the north end of King's Cross Station and the entrance to the Gas Works Tunnel all lines were crossed by two bridges. Battlebridge Road went across the end of the platforms from where Culross Buildings are today and into York Way, but north of Battlebridge Road was another bridge called Congrieve Street, which gave direct access from the east side of the station to the Imperial Gas Company's Works. In 1911, after the Gas Works had been closed, the Great Northern Railway acquired part of the land from the Gas Works and Congrieve Street disappeared soon afterwards. After a further exchange of land and settlement with the Regent's Canal Company in 1918 had been agreed, the Great Northern Railway authorised Sir Robert McAlpine to build a new road over the top of the Gas Works Tunnel into York Way, which enabled Battlebridge Road bridge also to be demolished a few years later. The way was now clear to move the station locomotive depot to its present site immediately west of the tunnel entrance and to construct additional suburban platforms on the land formerly occupied by the locomotive yard.

The site of the new locomotive yard had once been a dock off the Regent's Canal for barges serving the Gas Works. Consequently 190 yds. of brick retaining wall some 27 ft. high, which had only been built in 1892, together with 23,000 cu.yds., mainly of London clay, had to be removed in order to level the site.

In 1922 the first of the Great Northern Railway Pacifics had been constructed and the opportunity was taken to provide a new 70 ft. diameter turntable so that these engines could be turned at King's Cross. This turntable, of the central balanced type, was supplied by Ransome & Rapier Ltd. and was fitted with roller bearings to the end rollers. Its installation was not completed until 1924. Until then every Pacific working into London had to be sent on the 8-mile round trip to Hornsey for turning on the 65 ft. diameter turntable installed on the down side at the north end of Ferme Park Yard; this had been put down in 1913 to turn Gresley two-cylinder 2-8-0s working coal trains between Peterborough and Ferme Park Yard.

Top: The main-line running shed damaged during the second World War by a bomb which fell on the area known as "The Continent", in the foreground of the photograph. (British Railways)

Centre: Class A4 No. 4485 Kestrel in wartime — grimy condition. Photographed in May 1945. (Dalziel Foundry/British Railways)

Bottom: Class N2 No. 4760 damaged in an air raid at King's Cross. (British Railways)

During the summer of 1929 the London & North Eastern Railway announced that the whole of the locomotive accommodation at Top Shed dating from 1850 was to be renewed. At that time the allocation of locomotives was 178, including ten Pacific engines. To enable the latter to be dealt with satisfactorily, the layout of the locomotive yard was also to be improved and additional tracks laid down.

The new shed accommodation would provide for 200 engines. The water storage tanks were to be enlarged from a total of 63,000 to 70,000 gal. capacity and five additional water columns installed. A modern sand drying plant, special pits for the removal of ashes, and a mechanical coaling plant of 500 tons capacity, along with new sidings for the loaded and empty coal wagons, would be constructed. The existing turntable, which had been extended from 52 ft. to 54 ft. diameter since its installation, was to be replaced by a new 70 ft. diameter table large enough to take a Pacific locomotive. A new additional wheel drop was to be installed, together with an electrically-operated 30 ton overhead travelling crane in the erecting shop. The plant and machinery in the shops were to be changed to electrical drive, the lighting to electricity, and the hot water washing out plant enlarged to enable all engines to be washed out with hot water. The carriage repair work would be transferred to the existing carriage cleaning sheds at Highgate and the carriage repair shop converted into a shed for 17 locomotives.

Although it appeared that the whole of Top Shed was to be rebuilt, this was never carried out. After the alterations had been completed the original buildings of 1850 remained largely intact until the end of steam traction. Many of the proposals were in fact carried out over the next few years, but the depot was kept in full operation throughout.

Whilst the eight-road main line Running Shed also remained largely as it had been built in 1862, the traverser at the back of the shed was removed and seven of the eight tracks were projected through into the Erecting Shop behind; previously a single track from the Running Shed had served the traverser and the repair shop. The small buildings and offices at the back of the Running Shed were demolished. Whilst this provided more room for locomotives to stand at the back of the shed, it opened the shed at both ends and made it more draughty to work in. A total of eight roads were retained in the Back Erecting Shop in place of the original eleven tracks. The seven roads at the south end of the original 1850 shed had been terminated outside the building over the years and inside the former Painting and Carpenters' Shop a large Stores had been constructed, also an Oil and Tool Store and a notice case corridor for enginemen.

The layout of the locomotive yard was extensively altered. The Midland roundhouse was demolished and the site used to lay out seven long parallel tracks with engine pits for standing and preparing locomotives. The old coaling plant in the same vicinity disappeared and was replaced in 1931 by a concrete hopper type,

Class A4 No. 4468 *Mallard* on an Up Express at Hadley Wood at the end of the War. Note the partly missing buffer, dented streamlined casing, and spectacle window which probably would not stay closed. (*J. R. Meads*)

along with its associated sidings on the south side of the depot on land formerly part of King's Cross Goods Yard. The 54 ft. diameter turntable was removed and a new 70 ft. turntable built on another site near the York Way viaduct close to the entrance to the depot and within a few yards of where the turntable had been in 1850. This work was not completed until December 1932. Until this new turntable was ready the Pacific engines could not be turned at Top Shed and every one had to be turned on the King's Cross Station locomotive yard 70 ft. turntable brought into use in 1924. Alongside the new coaling plant new ashpits were constructed. It was envisaged at one time that these would be wet ashpits, with the hot ashes dropped from locomotives straight into water-filled hoppers underneath, but lack of either space or finance prevented fulfilment of the plan.

The engine shed covered accommodation was not actually increased by the alterations, as the loss of the roundhouse was only partly offset by the capacity to stable 17 additional locomotives in the old carriage shop.

The original water storage tank of 45,000 gal. capacity behind the Repair Shop was not altered, but the 18,000 gal. tank outside the former Midland Shed was removed. A new water softening plant was constructed near the signing-on lobby at the south end of the office block and brought into use in 1934. The new sand-drying plant was completed in 1932 and was of the rotating drum type.

The additional electrically-operated wheel drop was installed in the Repair Shop, so that Top Shed now had two wheel drops and a new overhead travelling crane made by Royce Ltd. in the Erecting Shop; this was of 30 tons capacity instead of 20 tons previously. The two sets of sheer legs visible in many old photographs of the front of the Main Line Shed and in the yard had already disappeared. The old beam engine was dismantled and sent to York Museum having been in use for over 120 years.

The carriage repair work carried out at Top Shed since 1862 was transferred to the carriage shed which had been built at Highgate in 1880 in order that carriages should not stand in the open and deteriorate in the winter.

The forecast that the alterations would provide for an allocation of 200 locomotives proved a little optimistic. Locomotives were increasing considerably in length, and in latter years not many more than a hundred could be accommodated within shed yard limits. Although the allocation was much higher than this, fortunately not all of them were required to be on shed at any one time.

After these major alterations had been completed during the early 1930s, Top Shed remained largely as it then was, with only small alterations and essential renewals as they became necessary, until closure in 1963.

During the Second World War several bombs fell in the Top Shed area, but only one did any serious damage. This was a large-calibre high explosive bomb which landed in the area known as

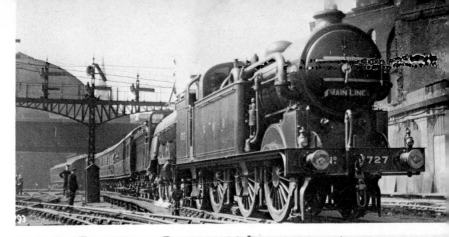

Top left: View from the top of the Water Softening Plant in 1952, showing the curved front original shed building on the left-hand side and the rebuilt main-line shed with a much lower roof. The North London line is visible across the background. *(British Railways)*

Bottom left: Top Shed Loco. Depot looking east in 1956. The coaling plant is included on the right-hand side, the ashpits adjacent. "Five Arch" with its many arches is in the background and carried Maiden Lane (later known as Brecknock Road and now York Way) over the King's Cross Goods Yard. *(British Railways)*

Top right: Class N2 No. 1727 is double-heading an Atlantic out of King's Cross to Potters Bar on a main-line express, a duty regularly performed on heavy trains before sufficient Pacifics became available. Battle Bridge, which spanned the platforms at King's Cross, is visible in the background, and on the right are the buildings of the Imperial Gas Works, which were demolished in order to build the Locomotive Depot on the site. *(Real Photos/ H. Gordon-Tidey))*

Below right: Three foreign locomotives on the Back Pits: Class B1 No. 61391, electric lighting dynamo on the right-hand running plate; Class V2 No. 60830 fitted with independent cylinders and outside steam pipes in place of the original monobloc casting; and Class A2/2 No. 60506 *Wolf of Badenoch* rebuilt from the Gresley Class P2 2-8-2. The gantry in the background carries the water supply which provided 1,000 gallons per minute for the locomotive tenders. *(P. N. Townend)*

the Continent, the name given to sidings which were alongside the main line shed on the south side. In addition to destroying some track, it demolished a large section of the wall and roof of the Main Line Shed. Several locomotives were damaged, including an N1 and a Gresley two-cylinder 2-8-0, but all were repaired and returned to service.

The running shed wall was repaired to match the rest of the building, but in 1949 the roof of this shed was extensively renewed at a much reduced height without the original profile. This altered the appearance of the 1862 building considerably, but the renewed shed roof did not last very long and soon required extensive repairs.

Towards the end of the Second World War a specially deep, white-tiled, electrically-lit pit was put down on the road that the Stirling eight-footer No. 1 had occupied for many years just inside the Erecting Shop.

The new pit was provided with portable weighing machines, which were kept in large wooden boxes. The intention was that the individual axles of locomotives should be weighed accurately and the springs carefully adjusted, but the pit seems to have been little used for the purpose intended, probably because it took too long to set up the weighing machines and only a limited number

of axles could be weighed in one operation. In 1956 Independent
Television visited Top Shed and a live programme went out from
the depot for an hour. The special pit, being rather cleaner than
those in the shed, was put to good use for the television camera-
men to televise the underneath examination of an N2 locomotive
before it left the depot to work in the evening service. The
fluorescent pit lighting was supplemented by high-powered spot-
lights, but during the examination of the locomotive drops of
water fell on them and one by one they were each extinguished
with a loud bang.

Along with other depots in wartime, Top Shed gained a staff
canteen at the rear of the premises but, unlike some others, it
remained in use for many years after the war. It was part of the
Shed Master's responsibilities to look after the canteen and it
made a change from locomotives to chair the regular meetings of
the Canteen Committee.

Early in the 1950's a much improved supply of softened water
was provided to the Back Pits. A steel gantry was constructed over
the seven roads with a feed bag for each track. A large-diameter
mains supply was arranged so that 1,000 gal. per minute could be
fed into locomotive tenders or tanks. As a Pacific tender held
5,000 gal., the time to fill its tank was reduced generally to under
five minutes.

An event of 1957 was that, for the first time for many years, the
proper floor of the main-line running shed was found. A cleaning
firm with special machine scrapers and scarifiers was called in and
two wagonloads of accumulated dirt and grease were removed
from the walkways between the roads.

Late in the 1950's both the Top Shed and Passenger Station
turntables were renewed. Both were worn out and the structures
had become distorted, making it difficult to turn large
locomotives without manual assistance. Two new 70 ft. diameter

Left: Cleaning the
accumulation of dirt off the
main line running shed floor
in 1957; an A3 class 4-6-2
provides the background.
(P. N. Townend collection)

turntables had been put down some years previously at such unlikely places as Melton Constable on the Midland and Great Northern Joint Line, and Witham on the Great Eastern Section. Dut to line closures these were surplus to requirements and had seen very little use. Although it was known that King's Cross would soon be dieselised, the two turntables were transferred from Melton Constable and Witham, and once more the task of turning locomotives easily with the vacuum tractors was accomplished. Some expensive track alterations were made in 1953 to enable tank engines to by-pass the turntable. This eased the flow of suburban engines into the depot, but there was still a bottle-neck at the coaling plant and ashpits at peak times.

After the diesel shunting locomotives appeared in the King's Cross Division in 1952, two roads in the Metropolitan Shed were partitioned off up to the roof level and made into a small diesel maintenance shed. A fuel supply was laid on from a storage tank in the Oil Stores and this shed was used for diesel shunter servicing and maintenance until the new diesel depot at Clarence Yard was opened in May 1960.

One of the new 75 ton steam cranes, constructed by Cowans & Sheldon in 1960, was allocated to the Breakdown Train at Top Shed. This displaced the 45 ton steam crane, which had been at King's Cross since being built by Ransome & Rapier in 1943. The 45 ton crane replaced a similar crane made by Cowans & Sheldon in 1940, which had been shipped to the Middle East and was said to have been lost at sea.

King's Cross was also supplied with a new Craven 35 ton crane during the First World War in 1915, but after the grouping took over a Ransome & Rapier 35 ton crane from the former Great Eastern Depot at Stratford. All these cranes, however, were a significant improvement over the 8 ton hand crane which was in use at Top Shed for very many years.

Below: A multiple mishap at Hitchin South, one of the many such mishaps cleared by the King's Cross and New England breakdown cranes and men over the years. The Hitchin L1 on its side was not involved in the collision, but it was stood there when the pile-up occurred and was knocked over. Usually such mishaps are cleared up by the following day. *(News Chronicle/Star/British Railways)*

4

Some of the earlier
Top Shed
Superintendents

In the first 75 years' existence of Top Shed only four District Locomotive Superintendents were appointed. Only one of them did not occupy the post for the remainder of his working life but went on to a higher position elsewhere.

The first Locomotive Foreman at the London station was a Mr. John Budge. He was appointed in July 1850 at a salary of £170 on a scale that ranged from £170-180. His salary increased quickly, however, and by 1862 it was £300 per annum but before then he had become known as the London Locomotive Superintendent. His responsibilities evidently were not confined to locomotives, as in 1866 he applied to the General Manager for an allowance of salary for the supervision of the farriery and harness repairs. The application was referred back in order to ascertain the number of horses shod yearly and the total cost thereof including materials. Probably this was the reason why the depot had such a large blacksmith's shop. Contiguous with the rear of the repair shop at the northern end were the sheds for the repair of road coal carts and no doubt John Budge, with his carpenters and blacksmiths, also looked after these.

The Board of Directors authorised construction of a house for Budge in July 1851, provided that the cost did not exceed the estimate of £380. This residence was situated behind the shed and separated from it only by the width of a roadway. In 1864 the house was extended at an additional cost of £175, but within a few years the Midland Railway extension had been constructed into St. Pancras Station, thereby isolating the house completely from the community of St. Pancras. The Midland main line actually passed within a few feet of the side of the house, and the nearby streets that had previously existed on the western side of the depot were all demolished. Nevertheless, whilst now surrounded by railway installations on all sides, the house remained in use for many years as the home of the District Locomotive Superintendent. Perhaps John Budge felt safer at nights, in what was then a rather rough area, after 1854 when the GNR decided to appoint an extra night policeman in order to prevent robberies

Top: Rebuilt Sharp's single No. 12 stands alongside the Main Line Shed with an unidentified supervisor — could it be Mr. Budge? *(I. Allan collection)*

Right: Two letters to Mr. Budge signed by P. Stirling. Copies were posted in the shed and at King's Cross Station, Hatfield and Hitchin. *(C. G. Woodnutt)*

Copy posted in shed & sent to Kep Hopfield

The Great Northern Railway
Locomotive Department.
Engineers' Office,
Doncaster 11ᵗʰ Decʳ 1868

Dear Sir

Mr Cockshott writes .
me that he has reason
to believe that Goods and
Mineral Guards occasionally
ride upon the Engine of the
train instead of in the Break.
This is contrary to rule &
I wish you to warn the
men in your district not
to permit the irregularity.

Yours truly
P Stirling

Copies sent to Mr & posted in shed

The Great Northern Railway,
Locomotive Department.
Engineers' Office,
Doncaster. Decʳ 23ʳᵈ 1868

Dear Sir

Some of the Passenger
trains are now being run
through the Hitchin Station at a
very high rate of speed.

I shall be glad if you will
issue a notice of caution with
reference to this, and direct their
attention to page 67 of Time
Table.

Yours truly
P Stirling

J Budge Esqʳ

at the nearby Horse Infirmary and the locomotive premises and offices.

In June 1866, just after midnight on a Saturday night, there was a multiple collision inside Welwyn North tunnel involving three goods trains and about 100 wagons which caught fire, making it impossible to enter the tunnel until 17 hours after the mishap. Flames were seen to emerge from the air shaft, the top of which was 80 ft. above the rails. John Budge, together with the Civil Engineer, Mr. Johnson, led a gang of about 450 navvies and mechanics into the tunnel in appalling conditions to make a way in for the fire engine and to clear the lines, which were re-opened on Monday morning for goods traffic and Tuesday morning for passenger trains.

There is no doubt that Budge exercised considerable authority over locomotive affairs at King's Cross. At times he communicated directly to the General Manager at King's Cross and not, as would normally be expected, to the Locomotive Engineer, whose office was originally at Boston and later at Doncaster. There certainly seems to have been some reluctance on the part of Stirling, after he had introduced his 8 ft. singles in 1870, to allocate one to King's Cross, as the first locomotive of this class to go there, No. 53, was not so allocated until November 1875, after eleven had been built and distributed elsewhere. This is said to have been due to Budge's preference for coupled wheels for the climb out of King's Cross to Potters Bar. Curiously, Kirtley, on the Midland Railway, had also taken the singles away from the Midland depot at King's Cross and replaced them with 2-4-0s before the Leicester trains were transferred to the new Midland line into St. Pancras Station in 1868.

The London depot was evidently short of locomotives in the 1860s, as John Budge was pressing over a number of years for more to be provided for general purposes and for working of local traffic. In a letter concerning the generally poor punctuality of King's Cross engines about this time Mr. Cockshott the Superintendent of the line was informed that Mr. Budge "furnishes as good an engine as he has at his command". John Budge also gave support to his staff, and on occasions memorials were submitted through him to the Directors asking for suitable housing to be provided for his workmen. One passed forward without comment in October 1872 sought a 10 per cent increase of pay and also for the staff to be paid weekly instead of two-weekly. Mr. Stirling was asked to look into this and recommended, tactfully, that where the rates of pay were below those of other companies an increase should be granted, but that a general increase should be declined. Both on the grounds of expense and because it would encourage improvident habits in the men, Stirling said that it was undesirable to adopt weekly payment of staff. Nevertheless, after it had been raised again by the staff at Doncaster Works, weekly payment of wages was adopted generally for the staff of the locomotive department in the following July.

In January 1884, Stirling reported the death of John Budge to

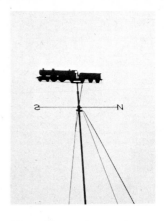

Above: The weather vane in the form of a large-boilered Atlantic, which was above the offices. *(British Railways)*

Above: Mr. E. F. S. Notter. *(Model Engineer)*

Below: The entrance to the signing on lobby and the offices in 1952. The general appearance had not changed since the days of Mr. Notter 40 years previously. *(British Railways)*

the Board of Directors and stated that he had held the position of Locomotive Superintendent since February 1855 to the time of his death. Evidently he had been redesignated Locomotive Superintendent in that year, but it is strange that no mention was made of his additional five years' service in charge of the depot as Locomotive Foreman. Mrs. Budge and son were allowed to retain possession of the company's house, and later a donation of £150 was made by the Directors in consideration of her husband's lengthy service.

David West was appointed from Leeds to succeed Budge at a salary of £325 + £25 allowance for a house. In 1894 his salary was increased to £400, and he retired in March 1902 with a sum of £500 presented by the Directors. Very little is recorded in the various minutes from David West, but it would certainly appear that his silence was well rewarded. However, he gave an interview in 1900, on the occasion of the visit of the Railway Club to King's Cross, when he said that he was responsible for 230 locomotives, whereas in 1860 only 40 had been allocated to King's Cross.

F. Wintour followed David West. He was allowed to live in the company's house rent free, but within three years he was appointed Works Manager at Doncaster, and additionally in 1915 Assistant Locomotive Engineer to Gresley with a considerably enhanced salary.

Wintour was the last Superintendent to live in the Locomotive Residence and the house was afterwards inhabited by the Assistant Locomotive Superintendent.

Perhaps the most well-known of the past King's Cross District Locomotive Superintendents was E. F. S. Notter, who followed F. Wintour, and remained there until his retirement in 1924. Notter was a railway enthusiast and the walls of his home, in Stock Orchard Crescent off the Caledonian Road, were hung with numerous pictures of locomotives and railway incidents. He was also a keen model engineer. At one time he was the owner of a large scale working model of a Stirling 8 ft. single, which he had rebuilt considerably himself, and which weighed about 2½ tons. This locomotive is still in existence. He also made a model of a Great Northern Atlantic, largely built by hand in the smoking room of his home, with the assistance of Mrs. Notter. H. N. Gresley was present at his retirement luncheon at Reggiori's Restaurant, King's Cross, and remarked upon his healthy and well-preserved appearance after so many difficult years at King's Cross. Notter would have been surprised to have known that his likeness remained in the depot until it was demolished. During his term of office his portrait had been grained into the wainscotting of his office wall just behind his chair, although it was said forty years later that he himself was unaware that this had been done.

About 400 members of his staff and their wives had attended a smoking concert at Alexandra Palace a few days before the luncheon at Reggiori's. A senior King's Cross driver, J. Wray, who took the chair, referred to many marked improvements that Notter had made at King's Cross during the time he had been

Superintendent. Specially mentioned were the messrooms for the general staff, the enginemen's room, the educational classroom, and the up-to-date office accommodation; it was added that the whole alterations had been carried out by Notter's own staff.

The same driver, Wray, had also presided over a ceremony 14 years earlier at which the new and well appointed classroom had been presented to the men by Reginald Wigram on behalf of the Directors of the Great Northern Railway in the presence of the Locomotive Engineer, Ivatt, and the General Manager, Oliver Bury. Despite the tribute paid to the Board for their generosity it is odd to see some years later that Notter had the room built by his own staff. A feature of the new classroom was that an excellent library was provided for the use of the men; the books were to be collected by a committee under the supervision of Ivatt to ensure that they would only deal with the men's calling. Many years earlier the Board had decreed that the money collected from the men in the Locomotive Department in fines for their misdemeanours should be used for the purchase of books for their education. Whether this still applied in 1910 is not known, but the speeches made did testify to the excellent relationships at the time existing between the company, its officials and the staff.

The appearance of the office building from the approach road through King's Cross Goods Yard took on its final appearance during Notter's time. The block of office buildings had been converted from shops used by various grades of artisans, and in 1910 a second floor was added to part of it for the classroom. Over the roof of this was a weathervane in the shape of a GN Atlantic, cut out of brass, and made locally by a fitter at the depot. The entrance to the timekeepers' lobby, where the men were booked on duty, was through a portico with two pillars bearing the name of the depot above them.

Class W 4-4-0 No. 1374 in the Station Loco. Yard after the shed had been demolished and the suburban station extended westwards. The print was used as packing behind the photograph of 4498 and *Sir Nigel Gresley* (reproduced later in the book) and only found when No. 4498 was removed for copying.

Arthur Smith, who was the Chief Clerk at Top Shed for many years and who retired in December 1969, was a junior in Notter's office. He had the job of taking letters down to the station each evening for Mr. Notter to sign. Although Notter visited the shed each morning, he then regularly went down to the station to see the 10.00 a.m. away and did not usually return to the depot. To sign the correspondence another small office on York Road platform was used, but Notter had a rule that he would never sign more than five letters each afternoon. If any more were taken down for signature they had to be returned unsigned to the depot. Perhaps this helped to reduce paper work!

Notter was responsible for about 1,600 staff. The depots under King's Cross at that time were Hornsey, Hatfield, Hitchin, and the GNR depot at Cambridge. Soon after the London & North Eastern Railway was formed in 1923 the separate Great Northern Depot at Cambridge was closed.

Some years later, in 1945, when J. Frampton was the District Locomotive Superintendent, the former Great Central Depot at Neasden with its breakdown area to beyond Aylesbury was included in the King's Cross District and remained under King's Cross until the line into Marylebone was transferred to the London Midland Region in 1957.

Upon the formation of the Traffic Manager's organisation at the end of 1957, the Peterborough district was eliminated and the Peterborough and Grantham depots were transferred to the Traffic Manager King's Cross. In this re-organisation the District Motive Power Superintendent, C. N. Morris, vacated his office at the depot, leaving Top Shed in the charge of a Locomotive Shed Master.

The Loco. Residence continued to remain in use as the home of the Assistant Locomotive Superintendent until bombs fell on the depot during 1941 and the Assistant at that time decided it might be safer to live outside London. For many years the locomotive turntable had been situated very close to the house. The noise of locomotives constantly banging the table up and down as they passed on and off it, together with the hubbub of all the other railway activities on the surrounding railways, made living in the house quite an experience, especially for little boys. It was the practice for the children of the household to be bathed in the room above the Mechanical Foreman's office in the Locomotive Erecting Shop, the hot water being fetched by the Shedman on duty from the nearby old locomotive-type boilers which supplied steam to the depot machinery.

After its vacation as a residence, the house was used as messrooms and changing rooms for the various grades of shed staff. By 1950 it had become so difficult to control, in its situation away from the principal activities of the depot and with the various nationalities involved, that instructions were given for the building to be vacated and demolished. Despite this, the house remains in use in 1974 leased as offices and is now the only surviving remnant of the GNR locomotive premises.

5

King's Cross
Locomotives

The first train out of the new main line station at King's Cross, which was opened on October 14 1852, left for York at 7.0 a.m. hauled by one of the Great Northern's ten newly-built Crampton single engines. These locomotives were soon found to be unsuitable for the gradients of the GN Main Line and were rebuilt by Sturrock into conventional singles. It had been agreed by the Directors that £50 per engine would be paid to Crampton for the use of his patent on the establishing of his patent rights to the satisfaction of Mr. Sturrock, as the first to be constructed had differed somewhat from the one specified. Later in the 1850s these locomotives, as rebuilt, covered the 32 miles from King's Cross to Hitchin regularly in 38 minutes at an average speed of 50 m.p.h. and generally averaged 60 m.p.h. from passing Hatfield to stopping at Hitchin.

In August 1853, Sturrock's large 7 ft. 6 in. single express engine No. 215 was delivered by R. & W. Hawthorn. This was a very expensive locomotive. It cost £1,000 more than the estimate, partly due to alterations requested by Sturrock during its construction, and Sturrock was called upon to explain to the Board why the estimate had been greatly exceeded. It had been built to gain experience with a larger type of locomotive than the GNR were then running and to rival the work of the LNWR "large Bloomers". It was intended to work passenger trains through from King's Cross to Grantham, instead of changing engines at Peterborough, and for this reason a large tender had been fitted.

Some doubts must have been expressed about the locomotive's performance in service, as again Sturrock was asked by the Board to report whether it was carrying out its work satisfactorily. He duly confirmed that it was, and also stated many years later that it did achieve the object of running distances of 100 miles at the highest speeds. This locomotive was withdrawn in 1870, although its driving wheels lived on for many years under a new Stirling single built specially to incorporate them.

In 1862 it was agreed to provide a pit and a water column at

Top: No. 1 "Little Sharps" single converted to a tank engine, a number of which were fitted with condensers for working over the Metropolitan Railway to Farringdon Street in 1863. *(B. Deer)*

Centre: No. 243A, a Sturrock Radial Tank engine built specially for the GN underground services in 1865. *(I. Allan collection)*

Bottom: No. 274, a Sturrock Radial Tank rebuilt by Stirling with a domeless boiler. The condenser vent pipe is in the bunker adjacent to the cab. *(I. Allan collection)*

Peterborough so that engines could work express trains through from King's Cross to Grantham, but it was not until 1876 that the regular running of Up and Down Scotch expresses over the 105.5 miles between London and Grantham without stopping commenced, in the commendable time of 130 minutes. For many years this was the only non-stop run over 100 miles in Britain.

In 1855 Queen Victoria travelled from London to Banchory by train, but the Queen's coach developed a hot axlebox at Darlington, necessitating her leaving the carriage. Two brake vans and a first-class carriage on the same train also suffered overheated bearings. Furthermore, a Mr. Haigh of the Locomotive department, who had been detailed to keep an eye on the hot axle in one carriage, fell off and was killed. Sturrock had some considerable explaining to do to the Board of Directors, but stated that the stock had been received at King's Cross from the Works two days earlier with the bearings in perfect condition. He had arranged for the stock to be given a trial run to Hitchin and back from King's Cross, but due to operating difficulties it had not been possible to run fast enough.

Between 1863 and 1866 fifty engines were introduced on the GN lines with steam tenders patented by Sturrock. The first three 0-6-0 locomotives thus equipped had been put to work in the London and Peterborough Divisions and had proved fully capable of working trains of 40-45 loaded coal wagons up the long 1 in 200 gradients, instead of the 30-wagon trains previously operated. Sturrock had agreed to let the GNR have the royalty on the steam tender patent at half price and the Board had stipulated that it was not to exceed £50 per engine. However, before all the engines on order with steam tenders had been constructed the instructions to fit them were cancelled. Sturrock retired at an early age to lead a full life for many more years as a country squire.

In November 1865 an unusual accident happened at King's Cross in consequence of a coal train running through the buffers

Above: A Crampton engine similar to *Folkestone* of the South Eastern Railway, worked the first train out of the new main-line station at King's Cross on October 14th 1852. The photograph dates from 1851. (British Railways)

Top right: Stirling condenser suburban tank engine No. 628 of 1879. Although bogie-fitted, it weighed no more than the Sturrock radial tanks. *(I. Allan collection)*

Centre right: The first 8 ft. 0 in. single to be allocated to Top Shed, No. 53, was not sent there until the end of 1875. It is standing at Belle Isle with a Stirling four-coupled passenger engine on the road used by locomotives waiting to drop down on to their trains at the Station. *(Loco & General Railway photographs)*

Bottom right: Stirling 8 ft. 0 in. single No. 668 working the 5.20 a.m. down passenger from King's Cross passing New Barnet. This locomotive participated in the 1895 railway races to Scotland. *(K. H. Leech collection)*

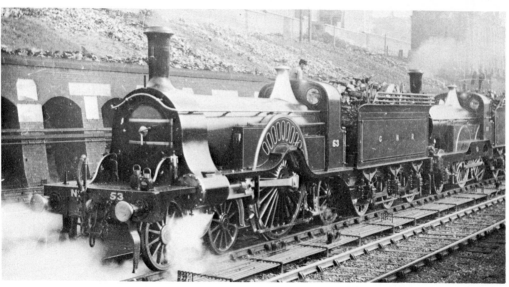

at the main-line passenger station, thrusting three or four wagons over the bank; one wagon was carried out into the road beyond. Meanwhile, the engine of the train had arrived in King's Cross Goods Yard! It appears that the driver had spragged his train at Holloway, then uncoupled the engine to enable him to move it about so as to supply water to the boiler — the practice prior to the adoption of injectors. On receiving the signal to start the driver removed the sprags, but forgot to re-couple the engine to its train before he started down the incline. At the points at the south end of Copenhagen tunnel the engine was turned into the Goods Yard, after which the signalman set his points right for the passenger road. In the meantime the coal train, which had been slowly advancing through the tunnel under Copenhagen fields, passed on through the Gas Works tunnel into the arrival line at the Passenger Station and collided violently with the buffer stops.

Many years later special hydraulic buffers with 7 ft. 0 in. rams were fitted to the five arrival roads and on a Sunday morning in 1904 some special tests were made to prove their effectiveness. A six-coupled goods engine with two close-coupled suburban trains attached, weighing altogether 369 tons, were run into each set of stops at speeds varying from 6 to 9.4 m.p.h. to the apparent satisfaction of Ivatt and the other officials present at the demonstration.

In January 1863, after much delay (some of which had been caused by the bursting of the Fleet ditch), the Metropolitan Railway commenced its passenger train services between Paddington and Farringdon Street with broad-gauge locomotives and stock provided by the GWR. A connecting line had been constructed from King's Cross Met. Station to York Road, on the Great Northern Railway at the north end of King's Cross Main Line Station, and the GNR had made preparations to operate through trains to Farringdon Street by means of this connection on September 1 1863. The Metropolitan Railway was the first Underground urban railway in the world, and the specially built broad-gauge locomotives were the first fitted with condensers, but these were not very successful as the tank capacity was too small and the water overheated.

Arising from a dispute with the Metropolitan Railway, the GWR gave notice on July 18 1863 that it would cease to work the Met. services at the end of September. The Metropolitan Railway decided to take over the running of these services itself on October 1 and the GWR retaliated by stating it would withdraw its trains on August 10. The Metropolitan Railway had, therefore, about ten days to find sufficient locomotives and stock.

Fortunately the line had been laid with three rails to a broad and standard gauge and arrangements were made to borrow carriages from the LNWR and GNR. Suitable locomotives were not so easy to find, however, as the Met. was precluded from emitting steam and smoke. The Great Northern had already started fitting some single tank locomotives with condensers and with these the GN intended to commence their own through services to Farringdon Street. Further locomotives, including some 0-4-2 and 0-6-0 tender engines, were hurriedly adapted by fitting a pipe and flexible tube from the exhaust pipe of the engine to the tender and about 12 locos in all were provided to work the Metropolitan Railway services. It has been said that Sturrock turned over Doncaster Works to make and fit the condensers in time.

The GW broad-gauge locomotives were still running the services on August 10, but during the following night the King's Cross crews carried out some practice train running to learn the road. On August 11 the standard-gauge service started, not without some anxiety as six derailments were experienced during the first day because the middle rail had not been used before and was found to be defective. The flexible condensing pipe also gave trouble, frequently bursting in service.

However, the difficulties were successfully surmounted and on October 1, one month later than intended, the GN started additionally its own "suburban and city" service to Farringdon Street. The Metropolitan Railway henceforth operated with standard-gauge stock and immediately ordered its own locomotives and carriages, which were delivered in the summer of 1864. The difficulties with the GWR were soon resolved and some through broad-gauge trains also were operated until 1869. The borrowed locomotives were returned to the GNR by the end of July 1864; the coaches had been returned a little earlier.

The GN locomotives had not been designed for continuous tunnel work. Even when condensing steam they emitted some smoke and fumes, which made conditions such that the crews are said to have requested and been given permission to grow beards as a protection against the fumes underground. On the other hand, it was also said to be widely recognised that the conditions were an excellent cure for bronchitis and asthma. Coke was used as fuel on the engines, although it was much more expensive than coal, but in 1868 Welsh coal was adopted. In 1874, Stirling thought that less obnoxious fumes and smoke would be generated by a reversion to coke, but no doubt due to its very high cost Welsh coal remained in use. One of the GN 0-6-0s provided also blew part of the roof away at Paddington Bishops Road when its boiler exploded upwards with some considerable force.

In 1866 the Great Northern and London, Chatham & Dover Railways commenced through workings with both passenger and freight trains. The GNR initially operated a passenger service to Ludgate Hill, but this was soon extended to Herne Hill, while the LCDR at first worked through passenger trains to Hatfield. Victoria was later substituted for Herne Hill, and Enfield, New Barnet or Finsbury Park became the terminating points of the LCDR services. The South Eastern Railway also operated a passenger service over the GNR between Greenwich and Enfield. All these cross-London passenger services had ceased by September 1907, but cross-London freight trains were worked from the GN line to various yards on the Southern Region until after dieselisation.

Left: Stirling 8 ft. 0 in. single No. 221 at the arrival platform, King's Cross Station. (British Railways)

Right: Stirling 7 ft. 6 in. single No. 872 on the "Continent" at Top Shed. No. 872 fitted with Ivatt domed boiler was still working on the fast light expresses non-stop from King's Cross to Doncaster in 1913. (E. Pouteau)

Below left: A King's Cross saddle tank No. 140A rebuilt by Stirling from an early Hawthorn goods tender engine. (K. H. Leech collection)

Below right: Stirling front-coupled mixed traffic engine No. 561 alongside the coaling stage at King's Cross Station. Platforms now occupy this site. Similar engines built over a period of 28 years were common on King's Cross to Hatfield, Dunstable and Hitchin stopping trains. *(I. Allan collection)*

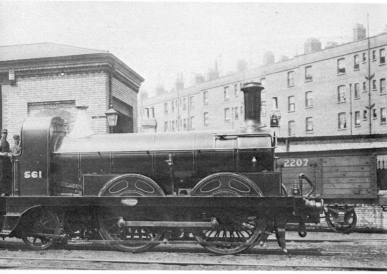

Bottom left: Stirling four-coupled passenger engine No. 262 waiting to leave the main departure platform King's Cross at about the turn of the century. Numerically Stirling built more four-coupled passenger engines than singles. *(B. Deer)*

Bottom right: The building of No. 990 in 1898 was somewhat sensational at the time and it was some years before it could be turned at Top Shed. No. 990 is passing Ganwick signalbox, long since demolished. *(Dr. Sellon)*

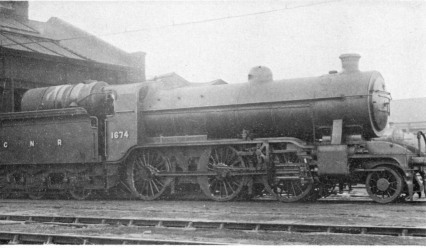

Above left: No. 271, at the rear of the coaling stage at Top Shed, was the only Atlantic with inside cylinders. (I. Allan collection)

Left: Oil-burning Ragtimer No. 1674 stands outside the main-line running shed during the coal strike of 1921. (M. Boddy)

Below left: The last of the Stirling suburban tank designs after being reboilered by H. A. Ivatt. The condenser has also been removed from No. 770. (I. Allan collection)

Above: A number of American 2-6-0s were brought from Ardsley in 1903 and tried on Enfield and Barnet trains from King's Cross. (*P. N. Townend collection*)

Below: Stirling suburban tank in York Road Station, King's Cross, waiting to drop down the hole to Moorgate. No. 933 was one of the last batch built in 1892-3. (*C. A. Lucas*)

In 1867 the GNR had appointed a French-speaking booking clerk at King's Cross York Road station in readiness for the start of LCDR Continental boat train operation from King's Cross, but no running of express trains via the connecting line appears to have commenced. For many years, however, the GNR timetables showed long-distance services in the reverse direction—for example, a departure from Victoria at 8.52 a.m. and Farringdon at 9.47 a.m. for Edinburgh, which were in reality the connecting train times for the 10.00 departure from King's Cross. In 1869 the GNR commenced their through services to the City terminus at Moorgate Street over the newly constructed and so-called "Widened Lines" of the Metropolitan Railway, which duplicated the existing lines from King's Cross Met. Station.

A number of the "little Sharps", which had been the first 50 locomotives put to work on the GNR in 1847 to 1849 as 2-2-2 tender engines, were converted to tank engines in 1852; eleven retained the single driving wheels, but one was rebuilt as a front-coupled 0-4-2 tank engine. A number of these engines were later fitted with condensers to work the GNR trains over the Met. Railway in 1863. Sturrock had asked the Directors if he could rebuild these engines, as many of their crank axles were breaking; he added that it seemed unlikely he could reduce either the speed of the trains or their loading. At that time authority to order some new singles for the main line was being sought. Sturrock offered to utilise the tenders off the Sharps rebuilt into tank locomotives for these singles: the £4,800 saved by not having to buy tenders for the latter would cover conversion of an unspecified number of the Sharps into tank engines.

Some of the rebuilds had also been fitted with radial axleboxes to the trailing wheels for easier negotiation of sharp curves; this was found particularly useful for working on the Metropolitan lines and in 1865 Sturrock ordered ten new 0-4-2 radial tank engines specially designed to cover the GN underground services. These engines were fitted with condensers and built to the reduced height of the Met. Railway loading gauge; the condenser consisted of a long pipe which ran below the footplate into the rear tank. Enough coke and water had to be carried in order to run through from Hitchin to Victoria.

Ten further locomotives of generally similar design but slightly heavier were built the following year. These engines are said to have performed a vast amount of hard work over many years on the services around King's Cross—albeit with some discomfort to the passengers in the leading coaches, which were subjected to considerable side oscillation transmitted from the engine. In December 1903 the last Sturrock well tank worked into Moorgate on a through train from Hatfield, where the locomotive had been shedded for many years to operate the branch to Luton and Dunstable.

In addition to rebuilding some of the little Sharps to tank engines, Sturrock had modified many of the remainder as front-coupled tender engines. In the early 1860s no other engines were

more in evidence on the local trains from King's Cross to Barnet and Hitchin. In addition they were used to pilot main-line trains to Hitchin when necessary.

For some years after 1866 the availability of engine power for the expanding local services out of King's Cross was an acute problem and timekeeping in consequence was far from satisfactory. Whilst the newly-built radial tanks were said to be doing their work well and keeping better time, at least five more engines were required for the steeply-graded lines to Highgate and Edgware, as these would not be worked well with old single-wheel engines.

John Budge, the King's Cross Superintendent, visited Hitchin in order to check the availability of the locomotives there after complaints about timekeeping in August 1866. He found 11 locomotives working and No. 21, a Sharps tank, the only one stopped, for a leaking firebox which was being patched. The locomotives were averaging 105 miles per day each. Budge complained that the depot had a mixture of coupled Wilsons, single Hawthorns, a coupled Hawthorn, tender-coupled Sharps and single Sharps, all liable to run the same trains, hence the unpunctuality. The position was so desperate that the engines had to take their shed days on Sundays only, as they could not be spared during the week.

The position at Hatfield was similar. Here 11 locomotives were running an average of 104 miles per day each. There was one spare single tank, No. 31, for the Hertford, Luton and St. Albans branches, two locomotives in shops, one for wheels and the other

Ivatt suburban tank No. 1534 is heading down the Main Line past New Southgate with a rake of eleven suburban coaches. *(I. Allan Collection)*

undergoing complete rebuilding; a shed day was being taken about every nine days.

Sturrock had called the Board's attention to the unsatisfactory position for engine power before he retired and Stirling had continued to press for authorisation of more locomotives. He also called attention to the 20 locomotives previously built without tenders on the Board's orders. The practice was to switch tenders from other locomotives under repairs, but Stirling rightly pointed out that this caused an unnecessary amount of fitting at depots which could be avoided if every engine had its own tender.

It was not, however, until 1869 that any more suburban engines for the King's Cross services were constructed, when 11 further 0-4-2Ts were built at Doncaster at the rate of three or four per year up to 1871. This batch of radial tanks differed from the Sturrock locomotives in having domeless boilers and inside frames for the coupled wheels. They remained in the London area until about 1910, in their later years being mainly employed on carriage shunting duties.

In 1868, when Stirling was considering the introduction of single-wheel express engines on the GNR, he arranged for the loan of one of R. Sinclair's outside-cylinder "W" Class 7 ft. 1 in. 2-2-2 singles from the Great Eastern Railway. No. 294, built by Kitson in 1865, ran express trains, with Driver Lloyd in charge, from King's Cross to Peterborough for some weeks. The first 7 ft. 0 in. singles that Stirling built in 1868 to 1870 had inside cylinders, but none of these engines were allocated to the London depot.

The first of the 8 ft. 0 in. bogie singles was built in 1870, but it was not until the twelfth was constructed at the end of 1875 that one was allocated to King's Cross. This locomotive, No. 53, was said to have been sent then to London specially to work the 10.00 a.m. from Leeds up from Grantham each morning. It had a near monopoly of that duty for some time.

For at least 15 years the Sturrock 2-2-2 7 ft. 0 in. singles, of which 12 had been built in 1860 to 1861, were the largest express engines in use from King's Cross and the design of these engines was generally considered as Sturrock's masterpiece. For some years until 1881 the first link at King's Cross had consisted of seven engines, including three of the Sturrock singles, Nos. 229, 235 and 240. By then the solitary 8-footer, No. 53, at King's Cross had been joined by Nos. 94, 544, 547, but the Sturrock singles took their regular turns with them in working the 10.00 a.m. Scotch express from King's Cross; this had been accelerated in July 1876 to run the 105.5 miles to Grantham in 130 minutes at an average speed of 48.6 m.p.h. In 1875 the scheduled time from London to Peterborough was 90 minutes, requiring the highest average speed on the GNR of 50.8 m.p.h.; the distance was frequently run in one or two minutes less. Three more 8 ft. singles, Nos. 666, 671, 774, went to the London depot in 1881 to 1885, but No. 547 was transferred away to Doncaster during the same period. The Sturrock singles, which had been rebuilt by Stirling, were then displaced from main line service, but continued to do fine work on

Above left: Ivatt
eight-coupled tank for
suburban working as built
with large boiler. These
engines proved unsuitable
for working into Moorgate,
and despite being reduced in
weight, the class were
relegated to coal trains in
the Nottingham area. The
large tanks of No. 116 were
ideal for advertising the
Great Northern Railway
services. (British Railways)

the Cambridge expresses until about the end of the century.

Stirling built some new 2-2-2 7 ft. 6 in. singles from 1885 and six were allocated to London, No. 229 in 1886, No. 230 in 1887, No. 872/3 in 1892 and Nos. 877/9 in 1894. Together with the six 8 ft. singles, these locomotives worked all the most important express trains from the London depot. No differentiation was made in the working of the two classes and Stirling himself regarded the 2-2-2s as more economical engines than the 8 ft. 0 in. singles. Speeds of well into the 80s were recorded by both classes, but the highest recorded speed, of 86 m.p.h., was achieved by a 7 ft. 6 in. single. The world record for the fastest booked express had been taken from the GWR in 1885, when a Manchester express was timed up from Grantham at an average of 53.6 m.p.h.

In 1895 two of the last batch of 8 ft. 0 in. bogie singles constructed were allocated new to Top Shed, Nos. 1007/8. By the following year the scheduled time of ten trains per day between King's Cross and Grantham had been reduced to 114 minutes. Out of the total of 55 runs over a distance of 100 miles non-stop in this country, the GNR worked 18 of them. The timing from London to Peterborough had by now been reduced to 83 minutes, an average of 55.1 m.p.h., but London engines still did not work beyond Grantham.

Right: No. 156, an Ivatt
0-8-2T, at Top Shed after
six of the class had returned
to King's Cross for working
empty coaches in 1919. The
condenser has been
removed. (I. Allan
collection)

Prior to 1898 a coupled engine was rarely seen on an express train south of Grantham, but the coupled engines, which were more numerous than the singles, did work the heavier stopping trains. The singles successfully hauled 150 to 240 tons at booked speeds of 45 to just over 55 m.p.h.

For many years in Stirling's time double-heading of trains was never resorted to, and he would not allow the front of his locomotives to be fitted with the appropriate brake connections. This policy had to be changed in the summer of 1894, when brake connections were fitted at the front of the singles, in order to improve timekeeping on heavier trains.

By the 1890s the weight of many of the express trains operated over the East Coast route had increased considerably with the addition of continuous brakes, toilets, heating apparatus, and the adoption of bogie corridor stock and dining facilities. Although the Board of Directors had asked Stirling to build larger locomotives to haul these heavier trains, he had responded by only slightly increasing the dimensions of the last batch of 8 ft. 0 in. singles. In fact, boilers generally appeared to have become smaller over the years, through a reduction in total heating surface.

Many locomotives had been constructed to the same basic designs throughout Stirling's long term of office. For example, the 0-4-2 mixed traffic tender engines, common on the King's Cross to Hatfield, Dunstable and Hitchin semi-fast and stopping trains for many years, were built in batches from 1867 to 1895.

Under the new Locomotive Engineer, H. A. Ivatt, the King's Cross motive power scene changed considerably during the next 15 years. Coupled engines appeared on many important expresses, though the use of singles persisted on the lighter trains and Ivatt

Above: No. 117, an Ivatt 0-8-2T, passing Belle Isle on a ten-coach suburban train of four-wheeled stock. The side tanks have been cut down in order to reduce weight. (Loco Publishing Co.)

Right: Rail motor No. 6 at Top Shed. Rail motors were used from Finchley to Edgware and on the branches from Hatfield and Hitchin. *(Real Photographs Co.)*

Far right top: The first Gresley three-cylinder 2-6-0 in Great Northern green livery stands in the Loco Yard at Top Shed. *(G. Marshall Smith)*

Centre right: Large-boilered Atlantic No. 273 working the 10.00 a.m. Bradford to King's Cross luncheon car express is taking water on the newly-installed water troughs at Scrooby in April 1905. *(P. N. Townend collection)*

Far right centre upper: The Royal Atlantic No. 1442 stands adjacent to 8 ft. 0 in. single No. 1 at the Imperial Exhibition at Shepherd's Bush in 1909; No. 1 was stored at Top Shed subsequently until 1924. *(I. Allan collection)*

Far right centre lower: Until sufficient Pacifics became available Atlantics were frequently double-headed to Potters Bar on trains of over 450 tons, and the Kings's Cross Superintendent in 1927 commented that the GN 4-4-0s were not much use for anything else. *(H. Gordon Tidey)*

Right bottom: Great Central 2-4-2T, LNER Class F2 No. 5778 at Finsbury Park. It is fitted for push-and-pull working to Alexandra Palace. *(P. N. Townend collection)*

Far right bottom: Top Shed Atlantic No. 1460 heading north on the "Harrogate Pullman" train at Belle Isle. Great Central four-cylinder 4-6-0s were sent to King's Cross after the grouping in 1923 and *Lloyd George* is waiting to drop down to King's Cross Station. *(H. Gordon Tidey)*

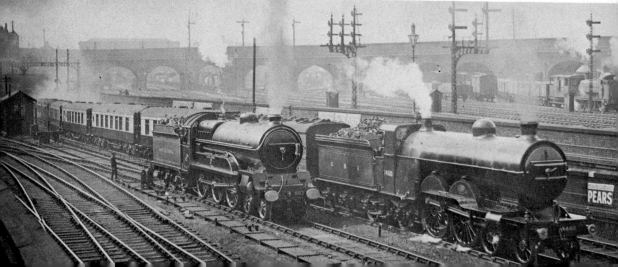

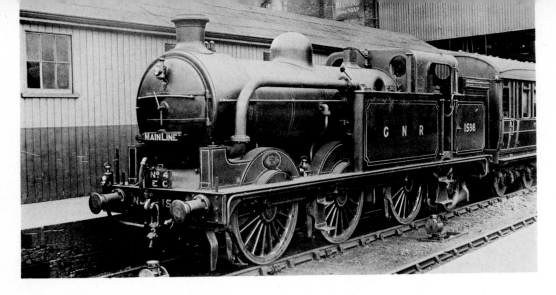

built 11 new bogie singles in 1900-01; two of these, Nos. 263 and 264, were allocated to King's Cross.

In 1899 the laying of water troughs had been authorised on the GN main line, but no troughs were provided between London and Peterborough until those at Langley were constructed in 1919 after some considerable delay in sinking a trial well, sanctioned seven years earlier. Water pick-up apparatus was fitted to the Ivatt 4-4-0s as well as to some singles and larger locomotives in the early years of the twentieth century; and this enabled non-stop workings over much longer distances.

The construction in 1898 of No. 990, the first Atlantic engine in this country, considered at the time to be a giant, was followed by the first large-boilered Atlantic late in 1902. Following the pattern set by Stirling neither of these new locomotives were allocated to London, and it was not until June 1900 that a turntable large enough to turn an Atlantic had been installed. Then, in 1903, new small-boilered Atlantics Nos. 252, 253 and 254 were allocated to King's Cross. By 1904 the Stirling 8ft. 0 in. singles were largely off main line work. A few went to Hitchin (including the last two allocated, Nos. 1007 and 1008), but the 8 ft. 0 in. singles were sometimes used double-headed from other depots on heavy expresses as late as 1907 if a larger engine was not available.

By 1911 22 of the large boilered Atlantics were allocated to Top Shed, Nos. 277-9, 299-301, 1400/14-16/26-8/40-4/58-61. The most famous of these was No. 1442, the GNR Royal engine, which had been turned out of Doncaster Works with bright rimmed tyres and beautiful finish to work the Royal Train to Leeds in 1908. During the following year it was exhibited at the Imperial Exhibition at Shepherd's Bush. The GNR coat of arms was hand-painted on each of the rear splashers. No. 1442's regular driver was H. Warren—"Mr. Warren" even to his colleagues—who was reputed to have had a liveried servant in his home. No. 1426, later 4426, remained at King's Cross throughout her career, as did No. 1459, which was one of the first to be scrapped.

LNER Class N1 Ivatt 0-6-2T fitted with a superheater. No. 1598 is on the No. 4 empty coach pilot at King's Cross in this photograph. *(P. N. Townend collection)*

From 1910 to 1913 Stirling 7 ft. 6 in. singles Nos. 872, 873, 876 together with Ivatt 4-4-0s Nos. 49 and 50 and Ivatt bogie single No. 263, were still hauling fast light trains, including the special Bradford diner express of four coaches, non-stop between King's Cross and Doncaster. The Bradford diner was worked by Top Shed engines and men to Doncaster and back in the day, 312 miles, on a timing of 165 minutes Down and 167 minutes Up. The Stirling singles had, however, been given domed boilers some years earlier by Ivatt. Whilst all the singles left King's Cross in 1914 it was not until 1939 that the last Stirling engine finally departed from Top Shed, when No. 4039, an 0-6-0, which had shunted Holloway Carriage Sidings for some years, was transferred away.

The Ivatt 4-4-0s were soon outclassed and in 1929 the King's Cross Superintendent Mr. J. F. Sparke observed that "they only serve a purpose when a train wants double-heading".

The last of the celebrated 8 ft. 0 in. singles had left King's Cross some years earlier than the 7 ft. 6 in. singles, with the exception of No. 1, which after exhibition with No. 1442 at the White City Exhibition had been stored at Top Shed pending planned exhibition in a glass case on King's Cross Station. This scheme did not, however, come to fruition, presumably because there was insufficient room anywhere to stand such a large exhibit, but No. 1 fortunately survived the First World War in a corner of the Repair Shed at Top Shed, though it had lost some parts and the firebox had become a shell. Late in 1924 it was sent to Doncaster and restored for the 1925 Centenary Celebrations of the Stockton & Darlington Railway. It was later exhibited in the Railway Museum at York. Then, to widespread surprise, in 1937 it was returned to service at King's Cross for a few weeks and achieved considerable publicity for the LNER by working a train of old GN coaches alongside the new pressure-ventilated train introduced in that year for the "Flying Scotsman".

By 1915 the Atlantics with their Top Shed crews were working from King's Cross to Leeds and back in the day, returning non-stop from Wakefield. The mileage of these turns totalled 371½ and was only slightly exceeded by other return workings to York, and for a short period to Harrogate and back, until the end of steam. The Atlantics had by then proved fully capable of handling trains of 450 tons out of King's Cross unassisted; a pilot was provided to Potters Bar only if that weight was exceeded. Considerably greater tonnages were worked beyond Potters Bar. In the Up direction, it is on record that an Atlantic hauled a train of 18 corridor coaches weighing about 600 tons gross from Peterborough to London in 92½ minutes at an average speed of 50 m.p.h.

In 1897 the working of the first fully vacuum-braked goods train commenced from King's Cross Goods, leaving at 3.25 p.m. and arriving Glasgow at 7.25 the next morning. The train was formed of 24 wagons, which consisted entirely of covered vans fitted with screw couplings with a brake van at the rear, and it was run at passenger train speed. The decision to operate faster freight trains had been taken because of the difficulty in pathing slow goods trains on Cup Final days over the main line, due to the large number of Football Specials run to the Crystal Palace.

Passenger engines were used on the fast goods trains in the early days, including the Atlantics, 2-4-0s and occasionally singles, but in 1908 to 1910 Ivatt built 15 mixed traffic 0-6-0s with 5 ft. 8 in. wheels and some of these engines were allocated new to London. Two years later a batch of 10 similar 5 ft. 8 in. wheel 0-6-0s, but superheated and fitted with piston valves, were built by Gresley. Those at London were used on the nightly through fast goods train to York as well as working excursions to Skegness and other relief passenger trains when required, sometimes reaching speeds of 70 m.p.h. Over 40 years later Hitchin was still using a six-coupled engine regularly on a morning suburban service to King's Cross.

Gresley's initial design of 2-6-0 followed and ten locomotives were constructed in 1912-13. A number of them were allocated to Top Shed for the fast fitted goods trains. The boilers of these locomotives were 4 ft. 8 in. in diameter, but the next batch which followed in 1914 had 5ft. 6in. diameter boilers although the leading dimensions including the grate area otherwise remained the same. The engines were commonly known as "Ragtimers", and officially by the LNER as Class K2. Several worked from King's Cross for a number of years on express as well as relief passenger and fast goods trains to Doncaster. During the Coal Strikes of 1921 three of the Class, Nos. 1641, 1671 and 1674, were fitted specially to burn oil fuel and thus operated from King's Cross.

In some observations made in 1918, Gresley stated that the fitting of larger boilers on the Atlantics and the 2-6-0s had produced more powerful locomotives. The big Atlantics, whilst identical with the first Ivatt design except for the boilers, had proved much more capable of keeping time with heavier trains, while the ten 2-6-0s with small boilers had consumed on an average of 5 lb. more coal per mile than those with the 5 ft. 6 in. diameter boilers.

In 1920 Gresley produced his third design of 2-6-0 built to the limit of the loading gauge and with a 20 ton axle loading. The class was known as the K3 in LNER days. Three cylinders and a 6 ft. 0 in. diameter boiler were incorporated, and for the first time the three piston valves were actuated by the form of two-to-one gear henceforth standardised by Gresley. The pull-out regulator handle fitted could be operated from either side of the cab. The locomotives were initially built by the GNR, but large numbers were built later by the LNER.

No. 1001, when new at Top Shed, worked a fast goods to Peterborough and back every day with her own driver. During the labour difficulties of that decade the K3 proved capable of handling passenger trains of 20 bogie coaches on the main line to Doncaster at an average speed of about 50 m.p.h. and could

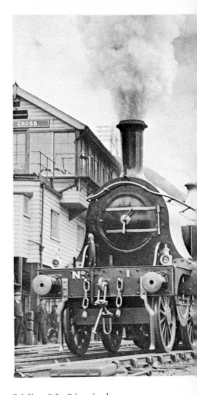

Stirling 8 ft. 0 in. single No. 1 made a suprise return to service in 1937 and is seen leaving King's Cross on a train of old Great Northern coaches. *(Fox Photos)*

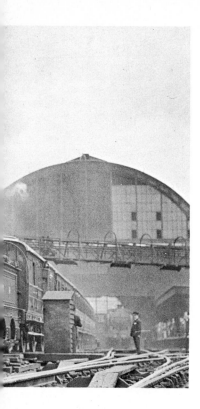

attain speeds of 75 m.p.h., as well as very successfully working the No. 1 speed fitted freight trains, for the haulage of which it had been designed.

By 1932 the Glasgow goods, which was the original fully braked train of 1897, had been accelerated by 100 minutes to produce a booked average speed of 39 m.p.h. throughout including six stops, this made it one of the fastest freight trains in the world. The load had increased from 24 wagons to 50 in the same period. There were now four fully fitted freight trains worked by K3s leaving King's Cross Goods Yard each afternoon and evening, running at No. 1 speed in railway parlance, and averaging 45 m.p.h. between stops, and seven partially fitted trains running at No. 2 speed averaging 35 m.p.h. hauled mainly by K2s.

The largest increase in the locomotive work of Top Shed, however, had resulted not from freight work, which was always small after Hornsey Shed had been built, but from the tremendous rise in suburban travel by the end of the 19th Century. In 1861, when Finsbury Park Station had been opened as a plaform at the point where the line crossed the Seven Sisters Road, three Up and three Down trains stopped there in a morning and five Down and four Up in an afternoon. In 1898 850 trains passed through Finsbury Park in a day and 40 complete train-sets were employed by the GNR on the suburban services, in addition to the trains worked through by other companies.

The provision of sufficient and adequate engines for the suburban services appears to have lagged behind requirements for many years. The complaints of the 1860's were repeated again in 1878, when Henry Oakley, the Superintendent of the Line, complained of the want of power of the four-coupled radial well tanks built by Sturrock and Stirling, which were not strong enough for the traffic to the south of London. Stirling had followed the construction of these four-coupled radial well tanks with some four-coupled engines fitted with bogies. This had resulted in transfer of the earlier Sturrock radial tanks to branch line work. Fitting of continuous vacuum brakes to the suburban trains had been authorised in 1878, after a train had run back on the Hotel Curve suburban platform. Further heavier four-coupled bogie side tanks were built up to 1895 and of these the 766 class, which were considered Stirling's best suburban locomotives, worked the through services to Victoria and elsewhere on the South Lines until 1899. In that year Ivatt commenced the construction of a large number of ten-wheeled tank engines fitted with condensers and cut down to the Metropolitan Railway loading gauge. The condensers on the Stirling and Ivatt side tank locomotives had been fitted externally from the smokebox to the top of the tanks instead of underneath the axles on the locomotives with rear well tanks. This simplified the removal of wheels as this could be done without dismantling the condensing pipe, but one of the Ivatt tank engines, No. 1520, had also an arrangement inside the smokebox whereby the exhaust steam pipes emerged at the bottom of the blast pipe immediately over the steam chest, which

enabled the boiler tubes to be removed without taking down the condenser fittings. The Ivatt ten-wheelers were still, however, only four-coupled engines and although they were said to do well on set trains of eleven four-wheeled coaches, no doubt they lacked the stamina required on the hardest turns.

Tests were made in 1903 with two of the engines coupled together on the Northern Heights branch in order to give better acceleration. Six-a-side seating had been adopted in the same year in order to carry more passengers. At the end of 1903 some of the American 2-6-0s were brought up to London from Ardsley, where they normally worked freight trains, and tried on Barnet and Enfield branch trains from King's Cross. Whilst they could pull 50 per cent. more than the locomotives usually employed, they did not remain long on the suburban services.

Two years previously Ivatt had introduced a successful class of eight-coupled mineral engines which became known as the "Long Toms". In 1903 a tank engine version was constructed and sent to King's Cross. This locomotive, No. 116, weighed 79 tons and was tested on a Sunday morning into Moorgate. The only difficulty experienced was with smoke from the cut-down chimney in the tunnels at King's Cross, but evidently other aspects of the engine disconcerted the Metropolitan Railway authorities. After being used on the King's Cross to High Barnet services for a time, No. 116 was soon returned to Doncaster Works, where it was fitted with a smaller 4 ft. 2 in. diameter boiler of the type used by Ivatt on the Stirling 8 ft. bogie singles and the side tanks were also cut down from 2,000 gallons to 1,500 gallons capacity in order to reduce the total weight to 70 tons 5 cwts. Forty more locomotives were built similar to the altered form of No. 116. but after a few years, due to clearance difficulties at Moorgate caused by their length and their general unsuitability for fast running, the whole class were withdrawn from the London suburban services and sent to Colwick for use on coal trains. Six of these engines with their large boilers refitted did, however, return to London in 1919 to work empty stock trains in and out of King's Cross, which duties they performed until final withdrawal in 1934.

In 1906 Ivatt built his last design of locomotive for the King's Cross suburban services, this time with six-coupled wheels and a pair of trailing wheels. The first engine, No. 190, was found to be too heavy. The side tanks were reduced in size and the weights redistributed on the later locomotives, in order to satisfy the Metropolitan Railway engineers. About 40 locomotives were built with condensers and used on the London suburban services. These engines, later known as Class N1, were particularly successful on the cross-London freight trains, which they handled for over forty years. The ten-wheel four-coupled Ivatt tanks, LNER Class C12, were not, however, entirely displaced on the suburban workings for a number of years, until after the Gresley-designed N2's had been built.

After twenty-five years or so in the country, a number of C12's returned to King's Cross without the condensing equipment, but

LNER Class C2 *Henry Oakley* leaving King's Cross local station. The small Atlantics worked the light Cambridge Buffet expresses in the early 1930s.
F. R. Hebron

fitted for push-and-pull working on the Finsbury Park to Alexandra Palace services. Here they displaced Great Central 2-4-2Ts of LNER Class F2, which had operated these trains since their introduction on a push-pull basis in 1942.

In 1906 steam Rail Motors had been introduced by Ivatt to work similar services on the Finchley to Edgware branch and off-peak trains on the Hertford and St. Albans branches from Hatfield and between Hitchin and Baldock. One of these Rail Motors was No. 1 and at one time the London division was in the unique position of having three No. 1's allocated — a Rail Motor; the 8 ft. 0 in. Stirling single stored in the Repair Shop; and an Ivatt 0-6-0 built in 1908.

After the grouping of the main-line railways in 1923, changes were made in the allocation of locomotives at Top Shed. The Motive Power Department was at first under a former Great Central Railway Officer and within a few months GCR four-cylinder 4-6-0 *Earl Haig* was transferred to King's Cross. This engine was initially employed on the 4.0 p.m. Down express to Leeds, returning the next day on the 10.15 a.m. from Leeds. In July 1923 the "Harrogate Pullman" service was inaugurated between King's Cross and Newcastle via Leeds, Harrogate and Ripon with a train daily in each direction. Several of the four-cylinder 4-6-0s were used on the Top Shed part of this working to Leeds non-stop in 205 minutes for the 185¾ miles, at an average speed of 54.3 m.p.h.

The Great Central 4-6-0's proved to be well capable of climbing the banks out of King' Cross and Leeds. Moreover, a maximum of 85 m.p.h. was recorded in 1924 by one of these engines on the Up Pullman. Nevertheless, there was no doubt relief among the regular King's Cross crews concerned in the workings when the class were transferred away from Top Shed in 1927. These engines were particularly heavy on coal and the GN Atlantics, which had deputised for them on the Pullman workings occasionally, took over all the King's Cross workings except for a short period in 1929 when a solitary Class D49 4-4-0, No. 245, was allocated to King's Cross.

The large-boilered Atlantics at King's Cross had by now been fitted with piston valves and large superheaters, performing their work most reliably and economically. Much publicity was given to the running times achieved by the King's Cross drivers when recovering lost time, which no doubt encouraged them to make even faster runs as the locomotives grew older. Many hundreds of miles were covered at speeds of 70 to 80 m.p.h. with these engines and a maximum of 93 m.p.h. recorded. In order to make up losses caused by a very late start from Leeds, Driver Payne of King's Cross with No. 3284 covered the 156 miles from Doncaster to King's Cross in 139 minutes with 295 tons in November 1933 at an average of 67.3 m.p.h; this was the first run from Leeds to King's Cross in under 3 hours in normal service. Not until the restrictions were lifted on Pacifics working to Leeds were the Atlantics finally displaced from the Pullmans in 1936.

71

6

Shed Work in the 1950s

The drivers of all locomotives, as they arrived on the depot under "Five Arch" (York Way runs along the top of the viaduct), reported in at the Bottom Time Office near the turntable and received instructions from the Running Foreman by telephone. Any repairs required to the locomotive were recorded by the driver on the repair card submitted at the same time. All tender locomotives would then proceed on to the turntable, which was 70 ft. in diameter and vacuum-operated.

The first turntable to be worked by the vacuum brake apparatus of a locomotive was installed experimentally at Top Shed in 1932. Prior to this, locomotives had to be centred accurately so that the turntable was balanced on its centre pivot; it was then pushed round by hand. This was arduous work, particularly in cold weather, and it was often difficult to balance the larger locomotives accurately as there was little room to spare.

The method adopted at King's Cross was for the locomotive vacuum pipe at either the front or back to be connected by a long flexible pipe to a small vacuum engine, which was mounted on a stand at one end of the turntable. This engine consisted of two oscillating cylinders and was geared to one of the race wheels of the turntable. As the driver created a brake with the vacuum ejector, the suction through the brake pipe caused the vacuum tractor to drive the turntable round through half a turn. A large vacuum reservoir tucked away underneath the turntable, which acted as an accumulator, provided enough power to turn a "dead" engine. Also, if required, the vacuum tractor could be thrown out of gear and the turntable turned by hand. The apparatus, made and patented by Cowans & Sheldons, proved very successful: its use was extended to King's Cross Station and employed on both turntables until the end of steam.

Tank engines bypassed the turntable, as they rarely required turning.

After turning, all locomotives proceeded to the coaling plant, which was mechanically operated and held 500 tons of coal in two

bunkers. Two roads ran underneath it and served four coaling positions. The hoppers were filled by wagons, which were hoisted bodily up the side of the plant on a table; at the top the wagon was turned over to discharge its contents. The wagon was not always emptied completely the first time. In consequence, some hundredweights of coal were sometimes left in the wagon if the operator did not tip the wagon a second time. Normally the coal hoppers were filled during the day turn of duty, but sometimes coal had to be put up during the night. This was all right so long as everyone made sure it was a wagon of coal, but on one occasion a wagon of long steel pipes was put into the Loco Coal Sidings by mistake and found its way into the coaling plant; they were very difficult to get out again!

To minimise smoke emission in the London area it had become the practice once more, as in Stirling's time, to use Welsh coal on the suburban locomotives and hard coal, generally from Nottinghamshire or South Yorkshire, on the main-line locomotives. The coal hopper was divided into two sections and by operating a movable steel plate either section could be filled as required.

Enginemen coaled locomotives themselves from steel operating cabins on the platform alongside the locomotive, which would be stood underneath one of the four chutes. The cabins were necessary for protection, as lumps of coal would sometimes fall off the top of the tender, which could be dangerous to anyone in the way. A fair amount was picked up off the ground each day, put in a wagon and tipped back into the hopper.

Generally these mechanical coaling plants were a boon and reduced the number of staff needed to coal engines very considerably, as well as eliminating the heavy hard work previously involved in coaling locomotives manually. Locomotives could also be coaled very quickly, in as little as three or four minutes. Difficulties were caused when the coaling plant required repairs or, occasionally, broke down without warning, as there were no means of coaling locomotives when the hopper had been emptied. In these circumstances arrangements had to be made quickly to hire suitable grab cranes, which coaled locomotives from the emergency coal stack or directly from wagons. However, grabs could not get into the corners of the wagons and the final emptying had to be done by hand. Also wagons were prone to damage when this method of coaling was used.

The type of mechanical coaling plant at King's Cross was eminently suitable for hard coal, which would pass through the hopper and still emerge on the tender as sizeable coal — sometimes too sizeable if it got wedged in the chute or in the tender coal gate when the locomotive was at work on the road. Such plants were not suitable for dealing with Welsh coal, which is friable and easily crushed. Welsh dust was hopeless for raising steam on a locomotive, as was discovered one day when an L1 locomotive received more dust than anything else; it was still on shed the next day raising steam. The fine dust would also make conditions at the

coaling plant difficult, to say the least, especially when there was a wind.

It was not unknown for locomotives other than the intended suburban locomotives to receive Welsh coal. At one time it was thought that Welsh coal might have to be used regularly on main-line locomotives in order to minimise smoke on the depot. Trials were carried out on an A3 locomotive and it was found that the locomotive steamed very well and extremely economically with a good grade of Welsh coal. No alterations were made to the grate or any other part of the locomotive. The coal consumption on this particular test was under 40 lb. per mile, but as the quantity of high-grade Welsh coal required was not forthcoming, hard coal remained in use on the main line—which was fortunate because much of the Welsh product would have been reduced to dust when it was tipped into the hopper.

One day the coaling plant attendant walked into the Shed Master's office with a leather satchel full of explosives which had come through the coaling plant and was found on a locomotive tender. The satchel was placed outside the door in a bucket of water until a policeman arrived and disposed of it into a nearby section of the Regent's Canal.

The only serious mishap which occurred with the coaling plant happened one Saturday morning when Driver Charlie Price went

Above: Class N2 No. 69524 is waiting its turn for coal, having by-passed the turntable. A wagon of coal is being tipped at the top of the hopper and Smoke Inspector George Mason has an audience of engine movement drivers.
(P. N. Townend)

Right: A4 No. 60028's tender being topped up with coal by Driver Stan Trigg and his fireman after making up the fire and prior to working non-stop to Edinburgh. *(E. Treacy)*

back for coal before leaving the shed to work the 10.00 a.m. "Flying Scotsman" with his regular locomotive, A4 No. 60010 *Dominion of Canada*. The practice of going back for coal was frowned upon, but resulted from the fireman's anxiety to fill the wide firebox up with as much coal as he could get into the back corners; this gave him a good start from King's Cross, but it also left a sizeable hole in the supplies on the front of the tender. The Running Foreman on duty at the main-line shed would watch the locomotive leave the front of the shed for its train working, but unbeknown to the Foreman the driver would sometimes nip back smartly on the arrival side to the coal hopper and fill the front of the tender again. If he was followed back by locomotives arriving on the shed, he would get blocked in and cause a late departure from the shed. The practice also resulted in overcoaling the tender well above the loading gauge. Some of the excess coal used to get levelled off going under the Regent's Canal inside the Gas Works Tunnel, but occasionally it would fall off on the curve through Hatfield station with serious danger to anyone standing on the platform; many times the wooden gate at the south end on the Down side was broken by coal falling from tenders. On this particular occasion, as Driver Price moved his locomotive back under the coal chute, which was made of steel plate, the chute tilted slightly. It just caught the top nut on the safety valve, which, on an A4 is inside the Vee front of the cab, and as a result, the safety valve casting was broken off at the base. No. 60010 had a full head of steam and an enormous fire burning through nicely on its 41.25 sq.ft. of grate. Charlie Price managed to get out of the cab, but was scalded badly; after some weeks in hospital he eventually resumed duty again. No. 60010 dropped the lead plugs but was otherwise undamaged. Despite many enquiries, no one ever ascertained why the coal chute tilted and fouled the safety valve at the moment the locomotive passed underneath.

After being coaled, locomotives arriving on shed then made a forward and backward movement to proceed to the ashpits, which were situated alongside the coal hopper. The ashpits at King's Cross were on three roads. They were emptied of ashes every day into wagons by means of a rail crane fitted with a narrow grab that went nicely into the width of the pits.

Firedropping was carried out by staff paid on a bonus system. Each class of locomotive had a time allowance, which varied from 30 minutes for a Class J52, 40 minutes for a B1 and 45 minutes for an N2, up to 80 minutes for the W1. When the times of the locomotives a man had put away aggregated 5 hours 50 minutes a bonus rate was paid. After an individual had completed what he regarded as his quota for the shift it was sometimes difficult to get any more locomotives disposed of until the next shift came on duty.

To be fair to the firedroppers, it was hard work under trying conditions and few men wanted the job. Most LNER locomotives were fitted with a drop grate on the front section of the grate, which was hinged and could be lowered so that the fire could be

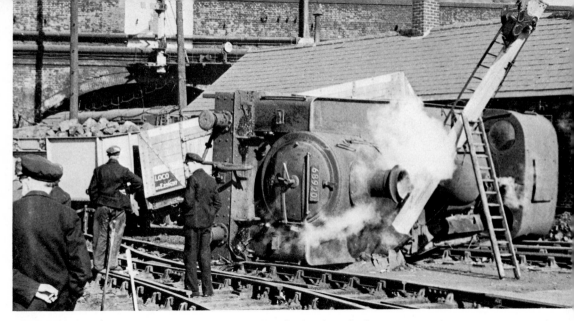

pushed through into the ashpan. The ashpan then had to be raked out. As the pits were frequently full of hot ashes, staff would try to empty them from the outside of the locomotive by raking through the wheels rather than go underneath. This resulted in ashpans not being emptied properly; sometimes they had to be washed out in the shed to clean them, which in turn caused more trouble as the drains quickly became blocked, the pits filled with water and no one could then work in the shed. Wooden clogs were a standard issue to firedroppers in view of the nature of their work, but they rarely lasted the stipulated time.

The later LNER Pacifics, B1s and British Railways Standard locomotives had rocking grates and hopper ashpans, which made the work of fire-cleaning and disposal very much easier. These grates gave very good service generally, but required renewal occasionally, particularly when damaged because fire had been allowed to remain underneath as well as on top; it was a heavy job to renew all the rocking gear as well as the grate.

Smokeboxes also required emptying of char on the ashpits, except on engines fitted with self-cleaning smokeboxes, which had

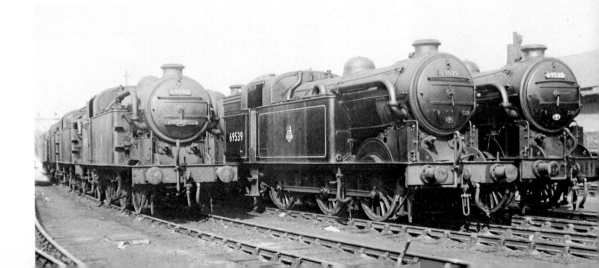

an "SC" plate on the door. On the L1 and B1 engines, most of which were supposed to be fitted with self-cleaning smokeboxes, it was common for the removable mesh screens to be missing. These were generally stored off the locomotive at the back of the shed, as the locomotives steamed very much better without them.

Engine tools, consisting of detonators, red flags, spanners, hand brush, oil feeders, etc., were collected in a bucket on the locomotive. After leaving the coaling plant, each locomotive paused at a small platform where the tools were taken off into the nearby Oil and Tool Store; here they were checked and replenished ready for re-issue when the enginemen came on duty to prepare the locomotive for its next working. This was a source of considerable difficulty, as tools invariably disappeared and yet no crew would leave the shed without a full set. Various methods were tried, such as painting the engine number on the bucket and the tools, but locking them on the engine where this could be done on the N2s and other regularly-manned locomotives seemed to work the best. When tools were in short supply — which in view of the number used was frequently — a crew could not turn their back on their locomotive, otherwise someone would nip up the other side and some item would be gone. Some years afterwards, when New England Depot was closing, a vast amount of engine tools was discovered; it was ascertained that Peterborough rarely had to order any, as the supply was always in excess of requirements!

Similar difficulties were experienced with short aluminium ladders, which were required to reach the footplate and the lubricators on Pacific locomotives, especially on the A4s, which had no front steps. If six were put out on the front of the shed for use during locomotive preparation work, they would have all disappeared within a day or two. It was later discovered that drivers were taking them about with them in their corridor tenders, so that they could be sure of having one next time it was required, usually at Gateshead the following morning.

The "cod's-mouth" keys also were difficult to keep on hand on the ashpits. Without one the streamlined front of an A4 — the "cod's mouth" — could not be wound open to get to the smokebox and empty it. The idea of using a handle on a shaft with bevel gears to open the front of an A4 originated with Corporation refuse carts at Doncaster. The arrangement worked well, needing little maintenance, but the keys were generally thrown down on the ashpits after use and no doubt many were picked up by the steam grab crane and disposed of with the ashes at Connington Tip.

Before it left the ashpit area, an engine's sandboxes were replenished with dry sand. In later years a Kelbus plant was used to dry the sand; such plants had become standard at depots in place of the rotating drum and other types, as their operation was much simpler. Once the hopper was filled with wet sand and the fire lit underneath on the grate provided, the sand would fall through to the hopper beneath by gravity through a sloping mesh screen which segregated and ran off any stones. The plant

The loco. coal was worked in daily by a Hornsey J50. On this occasion No. 68920 failed to stop and was derailed just outside the depot. *(T. A. Greaves)*

The Back Pits on a Sunday morning when many of the sixty N2s allocated were not required at work.
(P. N. Townend)

Top Shed from the top of the coaling plant in 1956. There are over 20 locomotives in steam on this photograph and the emission of smoke required to be closely controlled. *(British Railways)*

required little attention until the hopper was empty. To encourage the sand to fall through, a knocker was fitted to the side; this was connected by a Heath Robinson arrangement to a treadle on the track alongside the Sand House. Each time a locomotive went by it knocked the sand hopper and encouraged the dry sand to fall through.

Before the end of steam traction abrasive fines came into use for sanding locomotives. These fines were produced as a by-product at a steel works in the Scunthorpe area. Their use eliminated the need to dry the sand and keep it dry, as the fines did not absorb moisture so easily. Supplies could also be obtained in bulk in Presflo-type wagons and blown straight into the storage bin or overhead hopper. After many years' use, abrasive fines are now no longer available.

After fire cleaning and disposal, locomotives were then generally placed into either of the two running sheds or on to the Back Pits. Locomotives that were to be prepared for their next workings immediately, including most "foreign" locomotives, were placed on the back pits, where they were prepared and watered in the open.

The Back Pits had been built on the site of the old Midland roundhouse and consisted of seven straight roads with pits and points at either end. A specially arranged water supply delivered 1,000 gal. a minute from an overhead gantry that spanned all the back pit roads. The Pacific tenders held 5,000 gal. and could be filled in a few minutes, but more than 12,000 gal. might be evaporated on a run from King's Cross to Edinburgh and therefore considerable reliance was placed on the water pick-up gear.

The water scoop had a thin sheet steel snout section, which was fastened to the bottom of the hinged casting that could be raised and lowered by the operation of a hand-wheel in the cab. It was essential to check this snout every day and to renew it if it was found to be crumpled. Damage to the scoop was incurred if the fireman did not raise it quickly enough at the end of the water troughs, particularly at those locations with points or crossings nearby. The hand-wheel which operated the water scoop was similar to the one which applied and released the hand-brake, and sometimes new entrants to the footplate grade would operate the wrong wheel and lower the scoop by mistake. The wooden trunking and sleeper crossings about the shed would then be picked up, with consequent damage to the scoop when someone moved the locomotive. A wooden gauge, which went across the rails, was used periodically to check the operating level of the water scoop. The locomotive working the "Elizabethan" non-stop to Edinburgh usually had its scoop set an extra half-an-inch lower than normal; in practice this lower setting became standard on all King's Cross locomotives, as there appeared to be no good reason why other locomotives working down the main line should not share any benefit.

All locomotives were examined by an Examining Fitter on

arrival on the Back Pits. These were key men, few in number, but very experienced at looking for signs of trouble. They were paid a small additional examination allowance above the rate of a fitter. It was usual to see the Examining Fitter walk round with a long wheel-tapping hammer. They were also issued with a miner's type helmet, incorporating a light fed from a battery pack fastened to the man's back, so as to leave the Examiner's hands free; as the batteries were rechargeable, they could be put on charge after eight hours and be ready for use again when he returned to duty.

In twenty minutes to half-an-hour the Examiner would carry out a general check of the locomotive for loose or missing parts. Generally the items missing would be small ones, like split pins, which secured nuts, but these could and did cause very serious failures if not detected in time. Although it was rare to find a wheel defective, it did happen sometimes. On one occasion attention was drawn to a V2 tender standing on the Back Pits. One of the tender tyres was found to be fractured right through and the two sections were actually standing apart. As it happened, this was easily visible, but the facture could easily have been at the top and hidden by the tender frame. The locomotive could not be moved very far in this condition without the tyre coming off completely; most probably it had fractured through whilst the locomotive was standing on the depot. On the very rare occasion when a tyre fractured it was usual for the batch of tyres to be traced and each one changed immediately as a precaution.

The Pacifics occasionally were found to have fractured spokes,

Class A1 *Archibald Sturrock* being thoroughly examined by the shed examining fitters. This task was usually performed by one man but this photograph was posed for Messrs. Oldham & Son Ltd., the makers of the miners cap lamps. *(Philip Henderson & Co.)*

but provided it was only one or two the locomotive would remain in service under observation until called into Works. One day Class A1 locomotive No. 60149 was being put on to the wheeldrop road, having arrived at King's Cross unusually with a hot Cartazzi axlebox. As it was being shunted on to the wheeldrop road, the Cartazzi wheels dropped off the track. The axlebox cover was removed and it was found that the axle had been so hot that the journal end had been twisted off flush with the wheel; a length of the axle lay loose inside the axlebox. The cause of the overheating was that the drip pipe from the vacuum ejector had dripped water into the axlebox oil keep and the cure was to resite the pipe away from the axlebox.

After any repairs had been carried out arising from the examination of the locomotive, and any that had been booked by the driver from the previous working which could not be deferred, the engine was then ready for the engine crew to prepare it for the next working. This consisted of making up the fire, trimming the coal, filling the tank with water, and oiling round the engine. The driver was allowed a time of 45-60 minutes depending on the size of the locomotive for this work, including an allowance for signing on and time to read the notices. For many years it had been found that to avoid Pacific and V2 engines being late off shed, assistance in preparing these locomotives had to be given by another set of men.

The correct amount of cylinder and engine lubricating oil applicable to the diagram which the engine was to work was issued to the enginemen from the Oil Stores. Every diagram was worked out in miles and the issue of oil based on the total miles to be run from a chart provided in a Standing Order issued by the Motive Power Superintendent. The total amount of oil required by the driver on the larger locomotives did not usually bear the slightest resemblance to the calculated amount, however, and the driver invariably asked for more. In order to obtain the extra oil a chit had to be completed, then signed by one of the Running Foremen on duty and taken to the Oil Stores. The reason for this procedure was that at King's Cross it was the practice to fill the oil reservoirs and lubricators to capacity. How much oil each required was therefore more dependent on condition and how far the locomotive had previously worked than the length of diagram it was going to work next.

The A4s which worked the high speed trains from 1935 to 1939 were lubricated with a special lubricating oil. This was called "Silver Jubilee" oil and had a 25 per cent. rape oil content instead of the more usual proportion of 10-15 per cent. It was an expensive oil and was specially blended by Wakefields, but in latter years it was used as a standard lubricating oil for all the A4s to reduce the incidence of heated bearings. Arrangements were made to supply depots to which the King's Cross A4s worked, but this caused more difficulty insofar as the staff at such depots had to remember to use a different oil for a Top Shed A4. At one northern depot which turned round many King's Cross

locomotives the practice was to oil all engines of all classes in long lines. Several drivers were employed to do the job; one worked down the left-hand side of the line, and one down the right-hand side, and a third driver did the underneath work. It was doubtful if King's Cross A4s received any special attention in these circumstances.

The booked time of the engine to depart from the shed was half-an-hour before train departure time from King's Cross Station. It was intended that this should be the time the crew rang out to the signalman at Goods & Mineral Junction Signalbox, which was near the outlet signal. This was a long way from the front of the shed and constant supervision was required to ensure locomotives had actually departed.

A proportion of the locomotives at Top Shed, after being dealt with on the ashpits, required boiler washing out, heavy repairs or periodical maintenance examination. These engines had the fire put out entirely and were then set in either the eight road Main Line Running Shed or the five roads which remained for steam traction in the Metropolitan Shed, usually known as the Met. Shed. N2s were generally put in the latter shed. This was not an invariable rule, but the occasional Pacific which was stabled there looked a little out of place surrounded by N2s. Engines were set as far as possible bearing in mind the time they were expected to go out again, as both sheds were dead-ended and it was helpful to avoid unnecessary shunting of incapacitated engines. The two roads in the Main Line Shed, which served the wheeldrops in the Repair Shop behind, could only be occupied by engines requiring

quick repairs, as otherwise the wheeldrops could not be shunted.

Mechanical pinch bars were used to set engines a short distance. These pinch bars were made by a firm in Sheffield and incorporated a ratchet-operated shoe. The shoe was placed between an engine wheel and the rail, and the engine was then levered forward by one man. However, as the engine could only be moved about half an inch at a time, the use of pinch bars was limited and shunting locomotives were used if the distance to be moved was more than a few feet.

Top Shed had been provided with a hot water washing-out plant in 1909, and this had been extended and renewed in 1931 to serve both running sheds. As soon as a locomotive was placed in the shed the boiler blow-off cock could be connected by means of a flexible pipe to the system and the remaining steam and hot water in the locomotive's boiler blown down. Hot water was used to wash out the boiler and fresh hot water to fill up after washing out. Steam could be obtained again in a few hours, whereas with conventional cold water washing-out at least 12-16 hr. would be required to allow sufficient time for cooling down. The blowing-back part of the operation ceased after a few years, as some of the boilerwashing staff were rather apprehensive of the noise and writhing of the specially-made flexible pipes which, if one burst, could be highly dangerous. It was the practice therefore to blow the boilers down into the pit, but hot water was used for washing out and filling up. In the absence of blowing-back steam into the receiver, the hot water for washing out and filling up was heated by a stationary boiler.

A further difficulty experienced in the last years of operation with steam traction was that the various maintenance and servicing staff resisted working on hot engines and required the boilers to be cooled off with cold water in order to make working conditions more pleasant. This cooling could cause leaking tubes and fractured boiler stays if carried out too quickly. To cool down slowly, locomotive turn-round times on the shed were generally lengthened considerably if any work required to be done. In previous years an incredible amount of work had been done with pride on hot locomotives, or even engines in steam, and this had helped to achieve some of the pre-war feats such as running the "Silver Jubilee" with only one A4 locomotive every day for some three weeks until a second A4 had been built.

To improve the steaming performance of locomotives working long distances in the early 1950s, an instruction was issued at Top Shed that every locomotive travelling beyond Doncaster must have the fire out on arrival back so that the firebox and tube ends could be cleaned down, tubes swept, and also the boiler water changed. The instruction had been issued to ensure special attention for the locomotives working such trains as the "Tees-Tyne Pullman" to Newcastle and the "Elizabethan" to Edinburgh in summertime, and thereby improve the steaming conditions of the A4s. But it also precluded any attempt to provide a quick turn round to the locomotives, as they had to be cooled sufficiently for the Barman

The afternoon trio of A4s for the "Talisman", "Tees-Tyne Pullman" and "Yorkshire Pullman" being prepared on the front of the main line running shed. The "cods mouth" is open on *Wild Swan*.
(*P. N. Townend*)

to enter the firebox and carry out his unpleasant duties. Fortunately, when through engine workings became the practice again after 1956, a number of A1s were allocated to Top Shed, and the A4s were also being fitted with double blastpipes—soon extended also to the A3s—and as the steaming of these locomotives was thereby so very much improved the instruction could be conveniently forgotten. In any event double blastpipes had rendered the practice unnecessary, as "bird nesting" on the tube ends and blocked tubes then became a very rare occurrence.

Over a number of years before the Second World War, the LNER had gradually implemented a policy of softening the water used by steam locomotives over a wide area, which included the depots and water troughs on the main line between King's Cross and Doncaster. Previously water treatment had only been carried out at particular locations where the water was of very poor quality.

King's Cross had two sources of water, the original supply being taken from the nearby Regent's Canal. This source had been largely superseded in the last century by a mains supply obtained from the New River Company (later known as the Metropolitan Water Board) for locomotive purposes. This was of slightly better quality, but more expensive. In the year 1901, Top Shed was using 88 million gal. of New River Company water and 30 million gal. of the Regent's Canal supply annually. The station depot was using a further 104 million gal. from the New River Company.

When the water treatment plant was installed at Top Shed in 1935, the supply mainly used reverted to the Regent's Canal and

Four completely different front ends outside the shed. The small deflectors on A3 No. 60061 *Pretty Polly* were of little value.
(P. N. Townend)

was supplemented by the alternative Metropolitan Water Board supply when necessary. The station supply was also piped from the new treatment plant at Top Shed, which had a capacity of 40,000 gal. per hour and just under a million gal. of water per day. An attendant was on duty during the day to prepare the various mixes of lime and soda solutions used, also adding sodium aluminate, which would then last until the following day. The measuring and chemical dosing equipment worked automatically and was arranged on the ground floor. Above was a large diameter cylindrical steel tank. The raw water was fed into the top and mixed with the chemical reagents through an automatic distributor; the amount of chemicals pumped was in proportion to the amount of water passing through the plant and the water was suitably agitated to ensure an even density of the solution. The quality of the water was checked daily and reported to the Water Treatment Chemist at Doncaster. If any changes were required to the chemical mixes the depot was advised accordingly.

Periodically the plant required desludging and a suitable filter press was provided at Top Shed; this produced a solidified cake of white sludge, which was disposed of in old locomotive tenders at Connington Tip. One of these tenders came from a North British Atlantic. When the depot was demolished all the trackwork was removed but the Softening Plant remained in use for some time afterwards in order to feed the station depot. The North British tender was still under the sludge press, but stranded with no track leading to it, and eventually it had to be cut up on site.

Very occasionally it was necessary to empty the plant and clean out the interior of the tank. This was done about 1957, as it had been decided as a Regional policy to treat all water storage tank interiors with bitumen in order to prevent corrosion. A large overhead water tank had collapsed elsewhere in the Region with serious results a few years previously and had focused attention on the condition of all water tanks, some of which were over 100 years old. The sludge inside the King's Cross plant had to be dug out by hand, a difficult and unpleasant job for the staff concerned. The steel plates were found, however, to be perfectly clean and as good as new.

The use of softened water on a wide scale did considerably improve boiler conditions. The cost of boiler maintenance was reduced by the prevention of the formation of hard scale and corrosion; additionally, the wastage of the copper firebox plates caused by overheating due to heavy scale formation was prevented.

Locomotive performance was further improved by the introduction of polyamide soon after 1950. This chemical was added to the water in very small amounts and completely prevented priming and the carrying over of the boiler water into the cylinders. Polyamide was used by direct application into the main water storage tanks, if for any reason the water treatment plant was not working. Its use enabled drivers to work locomotives very much harder without the fear of lifting the boiler water.

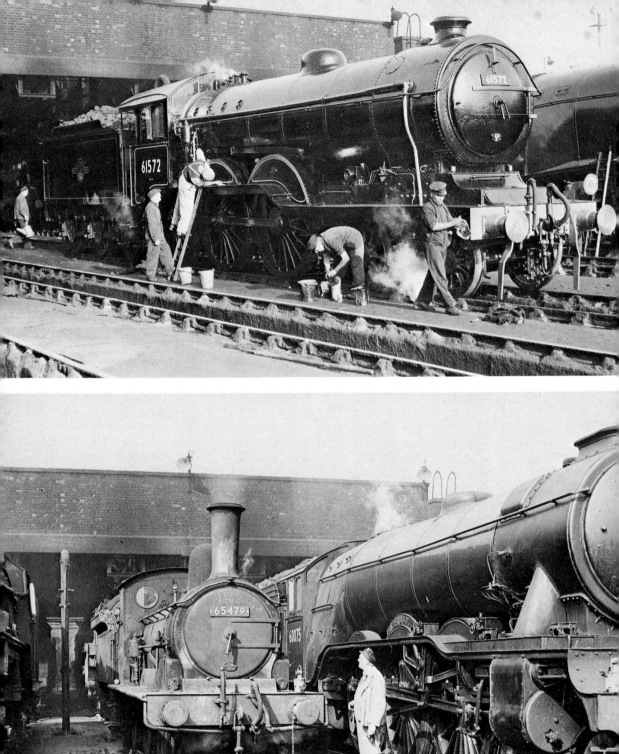

Theoretically it should have been possible to lengthen the periods between washing out boilers at Top Shed in view of the treatment given to the water, but the basic period remained at seven days for the Pacifics and about 14 days for N2, B1 and L1 locomotives. The N2s took water at a number of places in the suburban area where boiler water was not treated and the Pacifics and V2s also worked north of Doncaster, which was the extremity of the scheme completed by the LNER when war broke out in 1939 and effectively prevented further expansion of water treatment.

Boiler washing out was an important activity in the two Running Sheds in order to remove the soft sludge and any scale which may have formed. It was also necessary for the Boiler Examiner to examine the interior condition of the firebox thoroughly every two to three weeks through the washout plug and mudholes. At the same time the condition of the stays was checked and the examiner looked for any wasting of the firebox plates. A continuous record was kept for each boiler until the locomotive went to Works for overhaul and this was made available to the Chief Mechanical Engineer's Boiler Inspector, who also independently examined every boiler and its mountings most thoroughly at six-monthly intervals. Boiler maintenance on Top Shed engines, including the Pacifics, was very light. No special problems occurred in maintaining the large number of boilers with 220 to 250 lb./sq.in. pressure. The credit for this was due to the water treatment provided, together with the excellent design and construction of the boilers.

Much of the work of washing out and the examination of boilers was carried out during the morning shift, when the majority of the staff concerned were on duty. As the demand at Top Shed for Pacifics was heavy from 15.00 hr., commencing with the Niddrie Goods, which became a through working to Newcastle, careful planning and close supervision was necessary to ensure that after attention locomotives were in steam for their proper turns, many of which were regularly manned and required a specific locomotive. Steamraising was a difficult problem and was particularly concentrated in the early afternoon. In addition to the Pacifics required for the Down expresses, the express freight engines were needed during the late afternoon and evening and the N2s, L1s and B1s for the evening peak suburban services.

Raising steam could not be carried out without the emission of considerable quantities of smoke and conditions in the sheds after lighting up several locomotives were sometimes appalling. Both the St. Pancras Local Authority and the London County Council Sanitary Inspectors visited the depot regularly to ensure that no offence was being committed under the Clean Air Act. This problem was not new, as in 1909 the Great Northern had been served with eleven summonses and fined 40 shillings in two of the cases. The prosecutions had been brought by the London County Council "for locomotives which did not as far as practical consume their own smoke in the King's Cross Loco' Yard".

In 1956 it was an offence under the Clean Air Act if a locomotive in steam emitted smoke "darker than Ringelmann No. 2" for more than a few minutes. As the staff at the depot were ignorant of how dark this was, a Ringelmann chart had to be obtained. It had to be held alongside the offending source and so it was nailed to a long pole. The intention was that the chart could then be held in line with a locomotive chimney to ascertain if the smoke was causing an offence. The Shed Master and the Running Foremen were supposed to carry the poles around the shed with them and make spot checks on locomotives. Needless to say, this did not work very well as the pole was not very convenient to carry around; someone had to hold the pole whilst the Supervisor could stand well back and compare the smoke emitted with the grades on the chart.

Approaching the depot one day, I noticed that the factory-type chimney at the back of the Erecting Shop was emitting very dark smoke. This chimney had been erected for the stationary boiler, which supplied the water pumping machinery with steam in 1850, and it could be seen from afar. Suitably admonishing the man concerned, I added that the Local Authority could well prosecute in such cases. The offender replied laconically that he did not think so, as he was a member of the local council!

A more practical solution was to appoint a Smoke Inspector full-time to the task of educating the staff at the depot in raising and maintaining steam on locomotives with the minimum emission of smoke. George Mason came from Stratford to carry out these duties, which he did conscientiously until his retirement some time later. History repeated itself as many years previously in 1866 Mr. Sturrock had made a similar appointment in answer to the Board of Directors, who had received a complaint about smoke emission from the Marquess of Salisbury. Mr. Sturrock had replied to the Board that "he had recently put an Inspector for the special purpose of seeing drivers and firemen do their duty properly". About 90 years later, assistance was also forthcoming from the BRB in the form of their own London Inspector, Mr. Johnson, who was a former LNWR driver. He visited the depot regularly and entertained George with the exploits of various LMS and LNW locomotives. This liaison proved of value as the depot was informed of current affairs at other London depots on "foreign" Regions. One day we heard that Kentish Town was using on their "Jubilees" a firebox powder called "Xzit", which kept the tubes clean. The King's Cross lorry was soon round at this nearby depot borrowing a supply to try on the Top Shed Pacifics. One or two pounds of the powder, depending on the size of the locomotive, was sprinkled over the fire each time it was cleaned and made up. If used regularly the powder did prevent the tubes and firebox surfaces becoming sooted up; moreover, it helped to avoid the dropping of the fires on the Pacifics after long runs, which had been previously required in order to clean the tubes and fireboxes. The turnround of the locomotives was speeded up in consequence.

The firebox powder had another most useful property at Top Shed and that was to make black smoke white for about five to ten minutes after it had been sprinkled over the fire. This attribute was most helpful when the Local Authority Inspectors were on the premises, and supplies for emergency use were kept at strategic points on the Shed front. Even better results were obtained when the powder was made up into briquettes, which remained effective for a much longer period than the loose powder.

Despite the difficulties in getting engines off the shed to time with Council Inspectors frequently on the premises watching for smoke, the depot did manage to avoid prosecution and goodwill generally prevailed. In 1957 an approach was made from the Technical College in North London which trained the Council Inspectors on smoke abatement for a visit to the depot. This was so successful that it became a regular visit for each class, and the Council Inspectors were trained thoroughly and practically inside the fireboxes, smokeboxes and ashpans on the Pacifics at Top Shed.

When engines were lit up from cold there was a long period until steam was raised when a large volume of dirty yellow smoke was emitted from the firehole door as well as from the smokebox of the locomotive. It could be three or four hours before sufficient steam was generated to supply the jet ring in the smokebox and so disperse the smoke. Officially only two firelighters were supposed to be used to light up a locomotive, but as this was somewhat reminiscent of a Boy Scout's test of lighting a fire with one match, it was not surprising that the steamraising staff took a somewhat liberal view and interpreted this as two bucketfuls. However, their enthusiasm had to be restrained periodically as the quota of firelighters frequently ran out!

Use of hot water to fill up boilers in the Main Line Shed helped to reduce the time to raise steam, but to assist further some portable jet rings were manufactured at the depot. These could be dropped down the chimney and by means of a flexible pipe connected to the depot's compressed air supply. This air supply coaxed locomotives into steam in less than an hour, thereby reducing smoke emission considerably. Although it was contrary to instructions to force an engine into steam so quickly by this method, it was used constantly at King's Cross for the last five or six years and, although it was seen by the railway authorities, its prohibition was not enforced. No disastrous consequences befell the locomotive boilers through this practice and the problem of steamraising on the engines for the afternoon and evening services was considerably eased.

The planned maintenance of locomotives after 1950 was based on a preventative examination system. This was in accordance with a schedule known as Circular MP11, which had been developed by the London Midland and Scottish Railway and issued by the British Railways Board to all Regions. At Nationalisation the London & North Eastern Railway had a less complex system of periodical examinations in operation at depots, which included a shed day. However, the major examination scheme in use at King's Cross and many other depots was written on a single sheet of paper, whereas Circular MP11 filled 64 pages and was much more comprehensive, covering almost every component of all the locomotive classes on British Railways, including the different Regional designs and practices.

The Pacifics and V2s at Top Shed were planned to receive an "X" day examination every six to eight days, the B1, L1, N2 classes one every twelve to sixteen days and the few J52 shunting engines which still remained in service one every twenty-four to thirty-two days. A programme was made out towards the end of each week booking a fairly equal number of locomotives each day for an "X" day examination. When the engine came on shed usually during the night before the planned day, it was given a steam test and the various joints in the smokebox tested for steam tightness. The different parts of the locomotive operated by steam, such as the brakes, sanding gear, and cylinder cocks, were also checked for correct operation. After disposal, the engine was placed on one of the shed roads assigned for "X" days, the boiler washed out and the whole of the engine and tender components given a thorough examination. All repairs found to be necessary were booked on the "X" day card, together with any booked by the driver or deferred since the previous examination. It was a firm instruction that any repetitive repair bookings be given special attention.

The necessary staff were booked to carry out the required repairs and renew the brake blocks if required; particular care was taken to ensure that all fastenings were correctly tightened,

Chargeman Cleaner Dick Ball with his gang of cleaners, mainly of Polish origin, cleaning the engine for the "Elizabethan" and the locomotive which stood pilot, then worked to Grantham. No. 60010 *Dominion of Canada,* although in excellent condition, was not a successful choice for the non-stop and only completed one trip before *Seagull* took over. *(P. N. Townend)*

A fracture in the web of a Gresley built-up crank axle found on examination at the depot. *(British Railways)*

new split pins fitted where any were worn and that any locking devices were functioning properly. After completion it was laid down that the locomotive should be examined by the Shed Master or Mechanical Foreman to verify that it was in good condition and fit to run to the next "X" day with the minimum of attention.

King's Cross was fortunate in having as Chargehand Fitter Arthur Taylor, who conscientiously looked after the running of the scheme. Whilst the essential items were carried out as far as possible, the number of fitters of the standard required were not available in London and much of the success achieved was due to the hard work put in by the Chargehand. From the driver's point of view the scheme worked well. Many of the N2s and Pacifics were regularly manned and the drivers could defer booking any repairs until the planned day, putting up with any minor discomforts in order not to lose their own locomotive.

Many of the components of the locomotive were scheduled to be examined in greater detail at periods varying between three to five weeks and up to six months. Some important examinations were: the vacuum brake efficiency test carried out at three to five weeks; the renewal of fusible plugs in the firebox at seven to nine weeks; and the cleaning out and interior examination of tenders and tanks at six months. The examination of the moving parts of the engine were scheduled to be carried out after certain stipulated mileages had been run, commencing with the wheels and tyres at between 5,000 and 6,000 miles. At mileages of 10,000 to 12,000 the middle big end was due to be taken down and examined, also the coupling rods checked in position. At 20,000 to 24,000 miles the coupling rods were taken down for a more detailed examination and the Gresley conjugated valve gear was booked to be checked in position. The valves and pistons were removed from the cylinders at periods of 30,000 to 36,000 miles and a detailed examination of the cylinders and pistons made for wear and fractures. After this the cycle was repeated, the next valves and pistons examination being due between 60,000 and 72,000 miles.

Top Shed made some slight variations to the schedules which improved performance and availability. For example, the major examination was carried out between 30,000 to 36,000 miles and, although not booked at that examination, the conjugated valve gear was taken down and all pins and bushes renewed as necessary to bring the valve gear back to standard. As the valves and piston rings were renewed and the valves reset at the same time, it was considered better to do so with the two-to-one gear correct.

At a specified period, which was 15 months for a Pacific, 18 months for a B1, 24 months for a V2, and 27 months for an N2, each locomotive was proposed for Main Works repair. The locomotive would be externally examined and the visible condition of the various parts stated on a shopping proposal form listing all known defects. A recommendation was made on the form stating whether the locomotive required immediate attention in Main Works or whether it was fit to run for a stated period, usually between one month and six months.

The Shopping Proposal forms were received at the Chief Mechanical Engineer's Shopping Bureau. If the locomotive was accepted into the pool of locomotives for Works repairs, the depot was advised accordingly, but the depot was expected to keep the locomotive in service for a few weeks until called into Works. Frequently the Shopping Bureau would not accept the locomotive and sent the proposal form back endorsed, for example, "repropose in three months" or sometimes after a much longer period.

The intention of the system, which was operated throughout British Railways, was that locomotives could be shopped in an orderly fashion as their condition required and that long queues of locomotives waiting attention outside the Works, which was once the practice, would be avoided. Whilst it helped the Works arrange their intake of locomotives and also improved locomotive availability by reducing the time waiting works, the system did not always benefit a depot, which might have to keep a rundown locomotive in service for a further period. Although it was always said that shopping was based on the condition of the locomotive, this was often not so in practice; if the mileage run since the previous Works attention was too low, the locomotive would not be accepted unless some serious defect developed. With some classes of engine, suitable turns existed on which an ailing locomotive could be occupied: for example, an N2 could be used on a coaching stock pilot turn. But a Pacific, if not accepted for Works though in a condition unfit for main-line express work, was another matter. The tendency in 1956 was to resist taking the Pacific into Works unless over 80,000 miles had been reached since the previous classified repairs.

An example of a locomotive proposed and not accepted was No. 60044, a class A3 Pacific. As it was not fit to work an extended period, a further shopping proposal was immediately submitted and to bring things to a head, this stated that the locomotive would be taken out of service in a few days' time. The Shopping

Bureau arranged, as was usual in such circumstances, for the engine to be jointly examined by their own Inspector and the depot's Mechanical Foreman and a report submitted on the locomotive's condition signed by both parties. This achieved nothing in the case of No. 60044, as the Bureau's Inspector concluded the locomotive was fit to run on suitable work for another two to three months, to which the depot's representative countered that there was no suitable work for a Pacific with loose hornchecks and other defects and that it should be taken into Shops forthwith! As the mileage run by the engine was 70,000 and well below par, the Shopping Bureau still would not accept it.

Top Shed then took the locomotive out of service and put it on the Availability Return as "Waiting Works"! As the Shopping Bureau system prided itself on having practically no time shown waiting works, this would not do at all. All interested parties decided to visit Top Shed in force and examine the locomotive again in great detail. As the depot could not be persuaded to run the locomotive, a compromise was finally reached with the controlling authorities: No. 60044 was to be used on the Shed Pilot duty for a day or two, then it would be called into Works. This solution deleted the entry "Waiting Works", as the locomotive was theoretically put back to work. However, it was not very practical to shunt the shed with a Pacific, as visibility from the cab was not very good, and no driver would spend his shift reversing it continually as required in shunting work. The shed shunt driver was therefore instructed to book the engine number on his bill, whilst the locomotive remained dead at the back of the shed until called to Doncaster Works a few days later!

Top Shed was well equipped to carry out the normal type of depot repairs. Two wheel drops and an overhead crane could be used to lift and deal with hot boxes, or renew them if worn. If an A4 was getting rough and nowhere near due for Main Works, all six driving axleboxes could be renewed at the depot. King's Cross had been stopped at about the turn of the century from giving engines complete overhauls, but a visiting Inspector from Doncaster about 1957 was not very pleased when he noticed in the Repair Shop an N2 with tanks off and the boiler out of the frame. He quickly reported to the Chief Mechanical Engineer that King's Cross was carrying out a Main Works repair. Whilst the depot was admonished for having lifted a boiler, it was pointed out that actually all that was being done was to renew a broken stay, which was a normal depot repair but in an area which could not be got at properly without lifting the boiler. Another case later arose with A1 No. 60157, when six broken stays were renewed in the throat plate area, where they were sometimes prone to fracture on A1 locomotives. In renewing these six stays, more adjacent stays were found fractured and altogether 30 were renewed. This was well over the number that depots were allowed to renew in one boiler and instructions were received that no more stays were to be renewed on this particular locomotive; if any more factured it must be shopped immediately. At 197,000 miles this roller

Top left: The "Met. Shed" was the home of the N2s. (P. N. Townend)

Left: Class V2 No. 60902 waiting to work one of the York express goods trains from King's Cross. (P. N. Townend)

Centre left: A small number of goods engines came on Top Shed every day. No. 63971, an O2, was unusual in later years. (P. N. Townend)

Above: The back pits were used for locomotives in steam waiting and being prepared for their turns. Smoke emission was a constant problem. (P. N. Townend)

bearing A1 sustained another broken stay, so it had to be shopped — which just prevented Top Shed reaching 200,000 miles with one of these locomotives between classified repairs.

The various Running Shed activities were supervised by a senior Running Foreman, who worked an eight-hour shift and with his colleagues provided continuous cover throughout the twenty-four hours of the day. He was assisted by two Running Foremen on each shift, one of whom looked after the ashpits and the coaling of locomotives coming on to the depot, while the other arranged the setting of locomotives in the Running Sheds and on the Back Pits and also looked after the steamraising, servicing and preparation activities. All the Running Foremen were from the footplate grades and the senior men had many years of experience in supervising the depot. Their task at Top Shed had probably always been a difficult one because of the confined nature of the premises and the conflict of movements. There were times when so many engines were on the shed that it was almost impossible to move another locomotive until something departed. On occasions it was necessary to drop the fires on some locomotives and leave them in the Goods Yard until the depot could deal with them.

In addition to the physical limitations of the depot, the Running Foremen's duties were made more difficult after the Second World War because the nature of the work on steam locomotives was hard and dirty, which made it unattractive for recruitment of shed staff. There was a continuous intake of the unskilled grades, mainly among Commonwealth immigrants, but the turnover of staff was considerable as men left when they found what the work entailed, and the depot was rarely up to full strength. Some staff did become used to the work and after a time became reliable, cheerfully performing some of the hardest and most unpleasant jobs; but others caused their Supervisors endless problems. The total staff at the depot in 1956 was about 1100 and the wonder was that despite such problems of nationality, temperament and language the depot did function properly and maintained its standards to the end of steam traction.

Top Shed was fortunate in having an establishment of staff known as Shedmen Engine Cleaners. At most depots the cleaning of locomotives was undertaken by Engine Cleaners in the line of promotion to the Footplate grades of Firemen and eventually Driver. At peak times, as in summer, the Cleaners would be out firing on locomotives and no one would be available to clean engines. King's Cross had difficulty in recruiting sufficient boys for the line of promotion and rarely had more than a handful on cleaning duties. The cleaning of locomotives was mainly done by the Shedmen, many of whom were of Polish origin and had remained in this country after the last war. Some did not speak English and shed notices had to be translated into Polish; one Shedman who could speak good English was given a higher rate of pay to interpret instructions to his colleagues.

The Shedmen Engine Cleaners were divided into two gangs under their enthusiastic Chargeman Cleaners, Dick Ball and Harry Frost. Dick cleaned the main line locomotives and Harry the N2s and L1s. Both men had been at Top Shed for many years and took pride in their work. It was a pleasure in the late afternoon to see the rows of N2s, which had been cleaned in the Met. Shed during the day, and all the Pacifics for the later afternoon expresses lined up outside the Main Line Shed being prepared, looking very clean and in many cases with polished buffers and motion work. It was not possible to clean every locomotive, but there was one occasion when at about noon the depot was advised that the Prime Minister was on the 2.00 p.m. "Heart of Midlothian"; the locomotive had not been cleaned, but within half-an-hour of Dick being told it was looking fit to work the Royal Train.

Regular visits were made to Top Shed by representatives of various firms wishing to sell their products, many of which were proprietary cleaners or polishes. Most of these were expensive when used on the scale required at a locomotive depot the size of

Neasden was included in the King's Cross Division for many years, resulting in Neasden engines occasionally being sent over to Top Shed for repair. Class C14 No. 67418 is a push-and-pull fitted engine for the Chesham branch. *(P. N. Townend)*

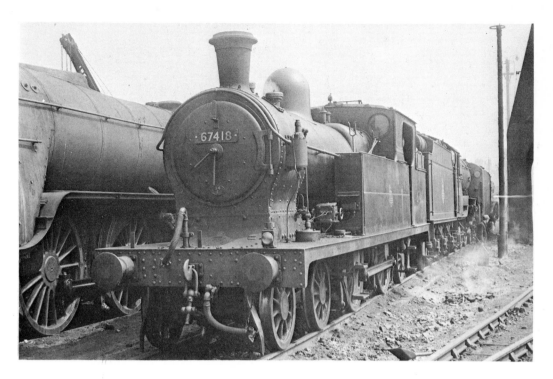

Top Shed, and some were not particularly effective.

One morning a representative was taken to an A3 in the shed to try his hand at cleaning the cab side. After much hard work the salesman said he had finished and that many of the marks would not come off as they were burnt into the paint by the heat from the boiler. It was suggested that he might like to have a walk round the shed. A little while later the cab side of the A3 was passed again, but this time there was no blemish on the paint-work and Dick was looking very pleased with himself. It did not pay to enquire too deeply into the methods used for cleaning, as the materials were found locally on the depot and did not always coincide with the products stipulated in the standing instructions.

On another occasion the A4 locomotive for the "Tees-Tyne Pullman" had not been lit up in time to have steam for the enginemen when they came on duty. They had to be given the pilot, No. 60020, which was a Gateshead Pacific due to return on a night sleeper at 10.15 p.m. The Chargeman Cleaner, immediately he noticed the change, insisted that the locomotive could not go on the Pullman as it was so dirty. The circumstances were explained: there was little option if the train was not to be delayed. A few minutes after the train had departed at 4.50 p.m. there was an outside telephone call to the depot asking if the Gateshead locomotive No. 60020 on the "Tees-Tyne" had been transferred to King's Cross as it had just been seen leaving King's Cross well cleaned! Rather than let it go out dirty on the Pullman, Dick had put every man he had on to cleaning it.

7

Some diagram and engine working arrangements

At Top Shed the Pacific and V2 locomotives were booked to their turns by the Shed Master personally. The Running Foreman on duty might have to vary bookings in the light of special circumstances, but in the case of particularly important trains, such as the "Elizabethan", he would telephone the Shed Master first. Each afternoon the Shed Master booked locomotives to the following day's diagrams, indicating engines for washing out, "X" day and periodical maintenance. The N2s and L1s were booked out by the Running Foreman's Assistant on duty, who was particularly familiar with the many diagrams for these locomotives. Booked records were kept of each locomotive's workings, so that the number of days worked since last washout, tube sweeping and "X" day examinations were quickly known.

The system of regular Pacific manning, covering all the important workings, was re-introduced at King's Cross in 1951. The principle of one driver to one engine had been common on most railways in the last century and Patrick Stirling had recommended this in his early years on the Great Northern Railway; but he had frequently found it necessary to share engines, which was unsatisfactory as both drivers would deny blame when anything went wrong. After the grouping in 1923, Top Shed had regularly manned certain Atlantics and Great Central 4-6-0s on many of the important trains, and later some of the Gresley A1s and A3s had their well-known regular drivers, but with the advent of the high-speed trains this could not be perpetuated and by 1939 a policy of common user locomotives was generally in operation.

In May 1956 nine A4s were each manned by two regular drivers. The driver on the longer-distance lodge turn to Newcastle or Leeds took his nominated locomotive in preference to his colleague, who would have to use another locomotive on a shorter-distance working. On lodge turns the locomotive generally worked down from King's Cross one day and up to King's Cross the next. The nine regular locomotives and their drivers were:

Locomotive No.	Name	Drivers	
60015	*Quicksilver*	W. Tappin	A. Clowes
60007	*Sir Nigel Gresley*	C. Simmons	W. Hoole
60025	*Falcon*	P. Heavens	T. Deeley
60003	*Andrew K. McCosh*	R. Turner	C. Willers
60014	*Silver Link*	A. Guymer	E. Hailstone
60017	*Silver Fox*	C. Graham	G. Tee
60028	*Walter K. Whigham*	F. Dines	A. Cull
60006	*Sir Ralph Wedgewood*	J. Edwards	A. Green
60022	*Mallard*	A. Smith	H. Smith

Wild Swan getting nicely into its stride, passing New Southgate on a Sunday morning express to Newcastle. *(P. N. Townend)*

The following table shows the locomotive roster as booked for a week in May 1956:*

Loco. No.	Sun	Mon	Tues	Wed	Thur	Fri	Sat
60028	"X"	3.50 4/45	Up	3.50 4/45	Up W.O.	3.50 4/45	Up
60017	12/18	Up	"X" 4/45	Up	3.50 4/45	Up	3.50 W.O.
60025		5.50 5/0	5.15 5/0	"X" 5/0	5.15 5/0	5.15 5/0	5.15 5/0
60007	W.O. 6/0	Up 7/21	5/30	Up 7/21	"X" 5/30	Up 7/21	5/30
60022	Up	W.O. 5/30	Up 8/20	5/30	Up 8/20	"X" 5/30	Up 8/20
60003	"X"	10.40 10/45	10.40 10/45	10.40 10/45	10.40 10/45	10.40 W.O.	10.40 11/0
60014		2.15 2/0	2.15 2/0	2.15 2/0	"X"	2.15 2/0	2.15 2/0
60015	W.O.	10.20 10/35	10.20 10/35	10.20 10/35	10.20 10/35	"X" 10/35	10.20 10/35
60006		12/18 W.O.	12/18 11/00	12/18 11/00	12/18 11/00	12/18	12/18
60030		9.10	9.10	9.10	9.10	9.10	"X"

Spare locomotives: 60034, 60026, 60032, 60013, 60021, 60029, 60008, 60044.

In Works: 60010, 60033, 60062.

Allocated: A4 Class 19
A3 Class 2

* Abbreviations used:—
"X" = "X" Day (planned maintenance examination) including boiler washout.
W.O.= Boiler washout.
. = a.m.⎫ For example, in the roster 3.50 is a.m. and 4/45 p.m.
/ = p.m.⎭ Both are train departure times from King's Cross.

The locomotive roster changed every weekend, when each locomotive number dropped to the next line in the table, the bottom one coming to the top again, and the sequence remaining the same; for example, in the list as tabulated, No. 60028 took the place of No. 60017 and No. 60006 the position of No. 60028 for the following week's roster. No. 60030 worked the 9.10 a.m. regularly at this time and was not part of the regular drivers' roster.

The following summarises the workings of the engines and men shown in the regular engine roster:

Diagram	Train Working	Back Engine Working
1	SX. 9.10 King's X-Leeds	5/15 Leeds-King's X
30	2.15 King's X-Grantham 2/0 King's X-Peterborough	7.30 Grantham-King's X 4/46 Peterborough-King's X
31	MWF. 3.50 King's X-Grantham MWF. 4/45 King's X-Newcastle	MWF. 8.26 Grantham-King's X TThO. 9.25 Newcastle-King's X
32	TThS. 3.50 King's X-Grantham TThO. 4/45 King's X-Newcastle	TThS. 8.26 Grantham-King's X WFO. 9.25 Newcastle-King's X

Right: No. 60025 *Falcon* working the inaugural Morning "Talisman" train on June 16th 1957, passing Holloway. The engine is already well notched up and the exhaust clean and dry. (*P. N. Townend*)

Below: *Seagull* and a smiling Driver Cull passing under the North London line on the express freight No. 266 Down to Newcastle. (*P. N. Townend*)

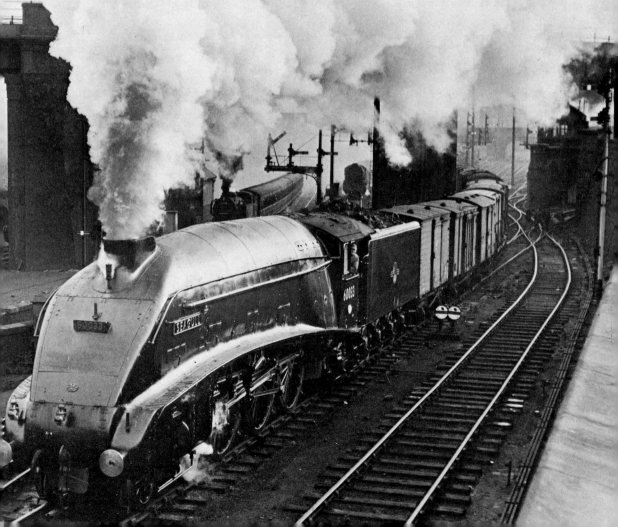

Right: No. 60103 *Flying Scotsman* leaving on the "Yorkshire Pullman" to Leeds after being fitted with a Kylchap double chimney. *(P. N. Townend)*

Far right: *Quicksilver* leaves King's Cross Station first stop Edinburgh on "The Elizabethan" — the longest non-stop run in the world. *(P. N. Townend)*

Below right: A4 *Woodcock* passing under the North London line at Belle Isle on "The White Rose" to Leeds. *(E. Treacy)*

33	5.50 (MO)	MO. 11.28 Grantham-King's X
	5.15 (MX) King's X-Grantham	MX. 9.27 Grantham-King's X
	5/0 King's X-Peterborough	9/40 Peterborough-Welwyn Garden City Goods
34	10.20 King's X-Grantham	2/44 Grantham-King's X
	10/35 King's X-Grantham	1.34 Grantham-East Goods (MX)
35	10.40 King's X-Grantham	3/39 Grantham-King's X
	MWO. 10/45 } King's X-	3.33 Grantham-King's X
	TuThFSO. 11/0 } Grantham	
36	12/18 King's X-Grantham	5/35 Grantham-King's X
	MO. 11/0 King's X-Grantham	Light Engine
38	MWF. 5/30 King's X-Leeds	TThS. 9.50 Leeds-King's X
	TThO. 8/20 King's X-Grantham	WFO. 12.4 Grantham-King's X Goods
	SO. 8/20 King's X-Peterborough	12.30 (Sun) Grantham-King's X
39	MWF. 8/20 King's X-Grantham	TThSO. 12.4 Grantham-King's X
	TThS. 5/30 King's X-Leeds	WFO. 9.50 Leeds-King's X
40	7/21 King's X-Peterborough	11/10 New England-East Goods
(6MT)		

Notes

Where SX is shown it indicates that the train did not run on Saturdays; TThO means that the train was worked on Tuesdays and Thursdays only, and similarly MWF indicates that the diagram operated on Mondays, Wednesdays and Fridays. 6 MT — adjacent to diagram 40 — indicates that a V2 could work this diagram. In most cases the men returned on the working shown for the locomotive, except in the case of the 9.10 a.m. which was worked by King's Cross men to Doncaster.

The following Down trains shown in the workings above were named as follows: —

4/45 King's Cross to Newcastle	"Tees-Tyne Pullman"
5/30 King's Cross to Leeds	"Yorkshire Pullman"
9.10 King's Cross to Leeds	"The White Rose"
12/18 King's Cross to Newcastle	"The Northumbrian"
2/0 King's Cross to Edinburgh	"The Heart of Midlothian"

In addition to the trains shown in the table above, Pacifics were required to work odd day trains such as the 1/5 King's Cross to Grantham on Mondays and Fridays only, and the 6/5 King's Cross to Leeds on Fridays only, returning on Saturdays.

.=a.m.   /=p.m.

A proportion of the locomotive fleet would always be under

Class A3 No. 60066 *Merry Hampton* passing Belle Isle on the occasion when Driver Fred Dines was trying out the engine whilst his own A was in Works. He averaged 90 mph for 23 miles on the return journey.
(P. N. Townend)

104

repair or undergoing major examination. Such locomotives would be covered for the number of days involved by one of the spare locomotives shown at the foot of the roster. The target availability for locomotives in traffic was 85 per cent., leaving 10 per cent. to cover repairs and 5 per cent. shopping in Main Works. In practice this was rarely achieved with the high-powered locomotives and day-by-day availability was generally much lower than the target, especially with the A4s. However, availability statements were somewhat nebulous affairs and the total depot figure usually came out somewhere near the target, albeit influenced by the very large fleet of 60 N2 locomotives allocated. A locomotive was counted as available for that day if it left the depot at any time up to midnight. The aim was therefore to get as many locomotives as possible booked out on the late evening turns after attention on the depot during the day. Top Shed had many late turns, which helped the depot to obtain better availability than it otherwise would have attained.

The nominated locomotives were changed when each locomotive went to Shops for overhaul, but frequently the regular drivers would eventually get their old engine back again. Locomotives were specially selected for the "Elizabethan" working each summer, and in April 1956 Nos. 60010 and 60033 had been specially shopped at Doncaster for this working. No. 60033 was the regular locomotive of Drivers Green and Edwards, but after working the "Elizabethan" for a period the engine was allocated back to them again. No. 60010 proved an unwise choice, as it only managed one trip on the "Elizabethan" and was in trouble for steam by the time it reached Potters Bar; but it managed to get to Edinburgh and back without losing time. Strangely No. 60010 always had a poor reputation for steaming and only lost it when fitted with the double exhaust system. No. 60033 had been fitted with the Kylchap arrangement when new and was always a winner on special workings such as the "Elizabethan".

The King's Cross locomotive working the "Elizabethan" went through to Edinburgh one day, returning the next day on the Up train. The Haymarket and King's Cross crews changed over *en route* by means of the corridor tender north of York and returned home the following day. A pilot engine was always prepared to cover the working and would then be used on a short-distance job to enable the engine to be back and stand pilot again the next day. The through engine working operated seven days a week, but the Sunday train was booked to stop *en route*.

The pride in the working of the "Elizabethan" was maintained until the train ceased to run at the end of the 1961 summer. It was rare for any time to be lost by the locomotive. For example, during the whole of one summer period the only locomotive failure was due to blockage of the injector feed supply by an obstruction in the tender tank, caused by a cloth being left in or dropped in by mistake; this caused ten minutes' delay changing engines at Newcastle.

The regular manning of the A4s worked very well and helped

everyone to get the best out of the locomotives at a time when many of the Pacifics were giving performances below their pre-war best. It did not put the inherent faults in the locomotive right, however; these will be discussed later.

The regular crews took considerable pride in their own locomotive and boasted about what it was allegedly capable of doing. One driver mentioned one day that he did not believe another well-known driver in the Top Link who had said that he had run the 44 miles from Darlington to York in 36 minutes. Yet a few days later he reported that his own engine was a better one as it had covered the same section in much less time!

At the start of the summer service in 1957 the locomotive usually run by Driver Fred Dines was in Works for overhaul. He was given an A3, No. 60066, which had been transferred from Doncaster only a few days previously for the summer workings. It was not usual at that time to run the A3s to Newcastle and as No. 60066 was somewhat unknown in its capabilities, Dines was asked to take the locomotive on the "Tees-Tyne Pullman" and back on the Up morning "Talisman" the next day, and to report how it performed. If he wished he could keep the locomotive until his own A4 returned from Works. The next day he reported that he would keep the locomotive until his own came back from

Driver J. Duckmanton leaving King's Cross Goods Yard on 266 Down freight to Newcastle with Class A1 No. 60157 *Great Eastern,* fitted with roller bearings. This was the most arduous of the King's Cross lodge turns to Newcastle. (*P. N. Townend*)

Doncaster, as it would do anything he wanted. Some time later an account of the run on the "Talisman" from Newcastle to King's Cross appeared in one of the railway periodicals. Passing Darlington 9½ minutes late, due to operating difficulties, he had managed, despite further checks, to arrive at King's Cross five minutes early having averaged 90.5 m.p.h. for 23.1 miles from north of Thirsk to approaching York and having reached 96 m.p.h. near Essendine. The net time for the run equalled the four-hour timing of the pre-war "Silver Jubilee", but with a heavier load of eight standard coaches.

About this time the practice of displaying the name of the driver on the cab side was revived. All the main-line drivers were given two small plates of laminated plastic with their names inscribed on them, which could be fixed on two small hooks on each side of the cab just below the rear window. Drivers were encouraged to hang up their nameplates in the hope that passengers walking by would become familiar with them, and that this would assist timekeeping. Many drivers soon lost the plates, but a few used them for some considerable time thereafter. Little if any reaction was noticed from the travelling public, however.

In addition to main-line passenger train workings, King's Cross locomotives and crews were responsible for a number of express

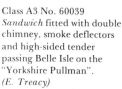

Class A3 No. 60039 *Sandwich* fitted with double chimney, smoke deflectors and high-sided tender passing Belle Isle on the "Yorkshire Pullman". (*E. Treacy*)

freight trains, including turns where lodging was required at York and Hull. The freight workings in May 1956 were:

Engine Diagrams	Class of Engine	Train No.	Train Working	Return Train
310/311	V2 6MT	268	2.30 King's X Goods-York	9/0 York-King's X Goods
		518 MO	2.40 - ditto - (MO)	
312/313	V2 6MT	714	4/5 King's X Goods-York (Dringhouses)	10.20 York-King's X Goods
				10.49 - ditto - (SO)
314/315	B1 5MT	666	8/30 King's X Goods-Hull	3/32 Hull-E. Goods
306	V2 6MT 2 engines	524	11/30 King's X Goods-Doncaster	8/30 Doncaster-King's X Goods
307	V2 6MT 2 engines	266	3/0 King's X Goods-York	12.28 TTh. York-King's X Goods
				1.30 WF. York-King's X Goods

.=a.m.   /= p.m.

There were also three short-distance freight workings to Hitchin and Peterborough.

The working of a B1 locomotive from King's Cross to Hull was unique in later years, as with so many wide-firebox Pacifics and V2s available on the main line the smaller King's Cross B1s were not usually called upon to travel any further than Cambridge or Skegness in summertime. The larger locomotives, however, were not permitted to work from Doncaster to Hull because of their weight and the lodge turn through to Hull had therefore to be a B1 duty. At holiday times the locomotive came back on an express train, which was the longest B1-hauled passenger turn on the Eastern Region. A B1 without the self-cleaning screens fitted inside the smokebox was a good locomotive and did the job well. Top Shed had an LM "Black Five" and several BR Class 5s allocated at various times, but the B1s were preferred and were the least trouble of any class of locomotive on this turn.

Above left: The Saturday morning "Butlins Express" to Skegness—a regular working for a King's Cross B1 in the summer. (P. N. Townend)

Below left: *Royal Sovereign*, a two-cylinder rebuild from the "Sandringham" class, regularly hauled an early evening train to Cambridge. Pre-war this working was carried out by one of the "Royal Clauds" from Cambridge. (P. N. Townend)

Right: LM Black "5" No. 44911 was allocated to Top Shed for some time in order to test the Automatic Warning System. The B1s were generally less trouble and preferred for the Hull lodge turn. (P. N. Townend)

Class N2 No. 69586 is leaving No. 16 Platform with a Gresley double-quad set which could carry nearly 700 passengers in the peak services. The train is the 5.31 a.m. from Moorgate to Hatfield.
(C. C. B. Herbert)

8

Suburban Workings

The express passenger locomotive workings undoubtedly attracted most of the public's attention at King's Cross, but the largest proportion of the depot's work was concerned with local operation. This included suburban passenger trains in and out of the three London termini — King's Cross, Moorgate and from 1945 Broad Street — empty stock workings, shunting and testing of coaching stock in carriage sidings, and a small number of local freight trains. By 1957 diesel-electric shunting locomotives had taken over all the goods yard shunting duties from the Great Northern saddletanks, the basic design of which had originated almost 90 years previously, but the rest of the local work after the last war had been carried out by the Gresley-designed N2 0-6-2 tank locomotives, assisted by some of the Thompson L1s.

The first N2 had arrived in London at Christmas 1920 and within a few months of the first reaching King's Cross, 50 were working on the London suburban services. The allocation of these locomotives to Top Shed was usually around 50 to 60 until dieselisation of the local services was completed over forty years later. The only competitor on local passenger trains after the N1s and earlier designs had been gradually displaced were a number of N7 class engines of Great Eastern design, which were built new for the GN suburban services in 1925. These were replaced within a few years by the construction of further N2 locomotives, though some of the N7s remained at Hatfield depot for use on the St. Albans, Dunstable and Hertford branches. The N7s had smaller driving wheels than the N2s and were not so suitable for the faster running required on some of the Great Northern trains, although for many years one did work regularly up to King's Cross non-stop from Hatfield each morning on a through train from Dunstable.

The N2s hauled passenger trains of eight closely-coupled articulated coaches specially designed for suburban work to Hatfield, Welwyn Garden City, various stations on the Hertford line and the Northern Heights branches, until the line to High Barnet and Mill Hill was electrified and taken over by London Transport in 1940. Although permitted on goods trains they were banned from passenger work on the single-tracked and curved line from Hatfield to Luton and Dunstable, which was why the N7 was used on the through passenger train each morning from Dunstable to King's Cross. The N2s with their high-pitched boilers, were considered unstable after some derailments in the West Riding of Yorkshire and were restricted in speed to 40 m.p.h. on the Luton line as a consequence; but this restriction did not apply on any of the workings in and out of King's Cross, on track which was generally well maintained and aligned. Speeds of 60 m.p.h. were easily attained where the distance between stations permitted; 50 m.p.h. could be reached in $1\frac{1}{2}$ miles from starting and 30 m.p.h. up a gradient of 1 in 60 with a load equal to 200 tons.

The GN suburban service was operated with considerable enthusiasm and alacrity. Station work was prompt and it is on record that an empty train has been run into King's Cross station, the inward engine uncoupled, a fresh one shunted on at the other end of the train and attached, brake re-created, heater pipes coupled, tail lamp, destination boards on the locomotive and blinds on the stock changed, several hundred passengers embarked, and the train got away, all within 70 seconds. Thus, $6\frac{1}{2}$ minutes after departing from King's Cross many of the passengers were alighting at Harringay, $3\frac{1}{2}$ miles away, within less than 8 minutes of the stock arriving in King's Cross station.

In 1929, 90 sets of King's Cross men were engaged daily on suburban work, together with ten crews from Hornsey and four from Hatfield. Although distances worked were short, one pre-war diagram required an N2 to cover 246 miles in about 20 hours, leaving the shed shortly after 5.00 a.m. to work the 6.11 a.m. from Finsbury Park and finishing at High Barnet at 1.02 the next morning, having worked nine times in and out of London to Cuffley, Gordon Hill, Hertford, Potters Bar, New Barnet, and High Barnet.

Most of the engines in later years were regularly manned by two sets of men who shared the same locomotive; generally one crew worked a train in the morning suburban service and the second set the same engine in the evening peak service. Some regular drivers were on these locomotives for many years, as not all crews wished to progress to main-line work. It was the practice of a number of the crews to keep their own engine clean externally for many years; some cab interiors resembled a jeweller's shop.

The N2 class had been specially designed to the maximum dimensions of size and weight allowed over the former Metropolitan Railway Widened Lines into Moorgate Station. They were not permitted to work the freight trains from Farringdon over Blackfriars Bridge to the Southern lines due to weight restrictions and in later years these trains had been covered by N1s and J50s from Hornsey Depot.

A succession of larger-than-usual locomotives had been built by the Great Northern Railway specially for the heavy work over these severely graded lines, but difficulties had invariably arisen

The Sturrock 0-8-0T of 1866 was the first of several classes which were found to be too heavy for use on the Metropolitan Railway. The two locomotives constructed spent their short lives shunting at King's Cross Goods Yard. *(Loco. & General Railway Photos)*

Class N2 No. 1763 in Great Northern green livery at Top Shed. Large numbers of these locomotives designed by Gresley were delivered in 1920-1 for the King's Cross suburban services. *(I. Allan collection)*

with the Metropolitan Railway after their construction. Sturrock was given authority in 1866 to order six big 0-8-0Ts specially for the Widened Lines workings, but only two were actually built by the Avonside Engine Company and these spent their short lives mainly on shunting King's Cross Goods Yard due to the restrictions placed upon them. Ivatt's design of 0-8-2T in 1903 and the first N1, No. 190, experienced similar difficulties, as mentioned in Chapter 5. Many years later when diesels arrived at King's Cross, history repeated itself; some types were found too heavy and barred from the Moorgate run and the Southern Region.

Within the physical limitations imposed upon their design, the N2s did excellent work, but much of their success was due to the skill of the regular men who operated them. If a new driver came into the link from elsewhere, usually it was quickly noticeable in the punctuality results.

Whilst the N2s had a fine turn of speed, particularly on trains which passed some of the local stations on the main line, they also had a certain reluctance to start from rest on a gradient, particularly where it was steep and curved like No. 16 platform (now No. 14) on the Hotel Curve at King's Cross. This was on the line coming out of Moorgate, which emerged through a single-line tunnel from King's Cross Metropolitan Station on a very tight, seven-chain curve and on a gradient steepening to 1 in 37 in the platform. The platform just accommodated an eight-coach Gresley articulated "double quad" set, which could seat 648 passengers with 12 in each compartment and sometimes carry another 200-300 standing. The south end of the platform was very narrow and consisted of a few planks which almost reached into the tunnel mouth. When a train started away from No. 16 platform it was common to see the driver leaning out over the cab side, watching the siderod as the engine was allowed to roll slowly backwards to the point of maximum tractive effort before the regulator was opened. If the engine would not start the first time, which was not unusual, the driver would drop back again, smartly reverse and have another try — usually with a nice snatch; but he could not set back for any distance as there were a pair of jack catches inside the tunnel behind him.

The 17.20 from Moorgate was probably the most heavily-loaded train of the day and became the subject of many delays and complaints. To try and avoid delays a Locomotive Inspector was frequently deployed on the end of the platform to try and help the driver stop in the best position for starting, but in the end it was decided to double-head the train from King's Cross to Finsbury Park every night. The timetable was not amended and to make up the time in attaching and detaching the second engine it was the practice to go hell for leather between the two stations. Double-heading a train regularly at King's Cross was rare and this was the only regular call for an N2 to be so worked.

The N2s were fitted with brackets at the front and rear to carry destination boards, which on an intensive service helped the passengers to know quickly where the train was going. This system had been adopted at the turn of the century and replaced a four-sided revolving arrangement. Each locomotive was required to carry a full set of these painted metal plates, which could be changed around by the crew to suit the various train terminating points, such as Gordon Hill, Hatfield and Potters Bar. The plates were painted locally and the painter was almost fully occupied keeping pace with the number which disappeared. As no one ever seemed to know how they got lost, the conclusion was reached eventually that the wind must blow them off the locomotive. However, one destination was eliminated about 1958 when the

Traffic Manager suggested that no visitor to this country would know where "Main Line" was; the hint was taken and no more plates with this destination were provided!

The N2s were also fitted with condensers to turn the exhaust steam into the side tanks when working through the tunnels around King's Cross and to and from Moorgate. A lever from the cab operated a flap valve inside the blast pipe. This was almost an impossibility to keep in working order for any length of time, as the blast pipe quickly coated with a deposit of burnt oil and carbon, which was difficult to remove except by burning out on a stand off the locomotive. The regular locomotives going in and out of Moorgate every day were no problem, because if the driver used the condenser it would prevent the flap getting made up. If he did not use it, he was not likely to book it as he would lose his regular engine. The spare locomotives were somewhat of a problem as the condenser, if not used for a few days, would not work when required.

Another special fitting on the N2s was the trip cock gear required by the London Transport authorities—it is used on Underground trains to this day. This provided a mechanical means of automatically stopping the train should the driver overrun a signal. The equipment was fitted in 1929 at each end and on opposite sides of the locomotive, so that the appropriate apparatus could be used in the direction of travel. In the Up direction, the fireman was required to get down at King's Cross York Road, set the trip cock arm in the "down" position and open the main isolating cock above, which connected the trip cock to the main vacuum pipe. The trip cock was usually known as the

Right: Class N2 No. 69592 passing Belle Isle for Hertford North as an A3 goes to the shed. *(P. N. Townend)*

Below: Class N2 No. 69505 without condenser double-heads the 17.20 from Moorgate on the 1 in 37 gradient from No. 16 platform to Finsbury Park. As no time was allowed for attaching and detaching the additional engine the locomotives went hell for leather between the two stations. *(P. N. Townend)*

Below right: Class N2 No. 69530 dropping down to King's Cross from the tunnel under Copenhagen Fields. The N2s almost invariably worked trains from King's Cross chimney north. *(P. N. Townend)*

"banjo" due to its similarity of shape. Coming out of Moorgate on arrival at King's Cross, the main cock had to be closed so that the apparatus was isolated on normal track. The trip was operated by a lever on the ground striking the arm of the cock, which then turned and allowed air to pass into the vacuum pipe on the locomotive should a driver pass a signal at danger. A similar requirement existed for locomotives travelling to High Barnet after London Transport electrified the lines, but locomotives working to the Southern Region, which also passed over the King's Cross Widened Lines, were fitted neither with condensers nor trip cocks in later years.

In order to check that the trip cock apparatus was in working order there was a tester at King's Cross Metropolitan Station and Highgate operated by London Transport. Every locomotive passing these two points was recorded and periodically strong complaints would be made that long lists of locomotives had failed the testers. Actually the tester checked only if the trip was set to gauge and not that the driver had opened the main cock, which generally he had not as the crew were worried about getting down amongst the live rails to reset the apparatus if it fouled anything at Moorgate or on the High Barnet branch. To verify that all the trip arms were set correctly, a wooden gauge was made at Top Shed which fitted across the rails and projected out to the required dimensions; against this locomotives were then checked periodically. However, despite this precaution locomotives still failed the testers and eventually an Inspector was sent out with the gauge to check the London Transport's testers. Both were found to be set at distances that differed from the gauge and from each other — which after much investigation was traced to the fact that the tester at King's Cross was for Metropolitan stock and the one at Highgate for Tube stock!

The only time the apparatus was known to have worked was when a train failed miles away from London with a vacuum brake defect and it was eventually traced to the trip cock having struck an object on the track; as the main isolating cock had either been left open at some time or shaken down, the brake had been applied. When this happened there was generally considerable delay, or even cancellation of the train, as no one thought to check the trip cock. The apparatus was really more trouble than it was worth, particularly for such a short distance of two miles from King's Cross to Moorgate, where the Widened Lines used were actually parallel to the London Transport electrified lines and the only lines electrified were in Moorgate Station itself. The apparatus also did not stop the occasional Midland line train from taking the signal incorrectly at King's Cross Met. and coming out of the wrong hole into King's Cross Station, instead of going underneath St. Pancras Station to the Midland lines. In such cases there was no quick way of getting the train back on the right lines and it had to be terminated at King's Cross.

For many years the N2s had given intermittent trouble by not steaming properly, due to the difficulty of keeping the Gresley twin-tube superheater element joints tight inside the smokebox. Commencing in April 1943, this type of superheater had been gradually replaced by the conventional Robinson 18-element single-header type, and together with alterations to the blast pipe the problem was overcome. In tests made from King's Cross to Hertford there was also a consistent saving in coal of nearly 2 lb. per mile in favour of the Robinson type superheater, on a coal consumption of between 46 and 48 lb./mile.

At the same time twelve locomotives had the cylinders reduced from the nominal 19 in. diameter when new to 18½ in. and one engine additionally to 18¾ in. No conclusions were reached and in practice many of the N2s had cylinders up to 20 in. in diameter after being successively bored out in shops.

Although the N2s were virtually free of inherent problems, serious failures did sometimes occur. Just after the start of the evening service one night in 1957 an N2 stuck with its train inside the Hotel Curve tunnel at King's Cross. The tunnel, being of single bore, was full of smoke and obnoxious fumes which could not be cleared and there was little wonder in the circumstances that no-one was keen to go into the tunnel and investigate the cause of the failure. After some delay it was ascertained that the crank axle had fractured right through and the failed locomotive had to be assisted out very slowly by another N2 on the front and an almost asphyxiated observer on the running plate. On such

Gresley twin-tube-type superheater fitted to the N2 class. Difficulty was experienced with keeping the joints steamtight and the conventional Robinson type superheater was fitted after 1943. *(P. N. Townend collection)*

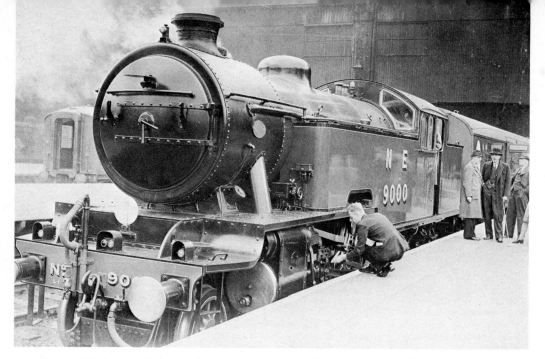

occasions, which were fortunately rare, the remainder of th_
evening service from Moorgate was cancelled, as dealing with such
failures took a considerable time and the trains behind could not
be released until the failure was removed.

The N2s marshalled main-line trains in the various carriage
sidings and also worked many of the empty coaches into and out of
King's Cross Station. After the war, the N2s were assisted in these
duties by the L1 class 2-6-4Ts designed by Edward Thompson,
and these larger locomotives additionally worked many of the
outer suburban trains to Hitchin, Baldock and Royston. The B1
class 4-6-0 tender engines also participated in the outer suburban
work and handled trains to and from Cambridge. The B1s were
much better suited to the fast running required on these services,
especially the Cambridge Buffet Expresses, which were sharply
timed and had a limited number of stops. Pacifics and V2s were
also frequently used on Cambridge trains in order to season the
engine after attention to the bearings or after main works
overhaul; the morning "Parly" at 6.5, stopping at most stations,
was particularly useful for this purpose. Two Fowler LMS 2-6-4Ts
found their way to King's Cross in 1956 and before being disposed
of to Hitchin successfully worked one or two Cambridge trains.
The L1s, however, were not regularly used to Cambridge, except
for a short period when the turntable at Cambridge was under
repair. Despite the early promise of the prototype, No. 9000,
working anything from express trains to heavy coal traffic, and
that speeds of 70 m.p.h. could be easily attained although the
driving wheels were only 5 ft. 2 in. in diameter, the class generally
gave better performances in the hands of Hitchin crews than with
King's Cross men.

The L1s were used to haul the heavy trains of sleeping cars out

The first Class L1, No.
9000, in resplendent apple
green livery being inspected
at King's Cross when new in
1945 by railway enthusiasts
which include Arthur Cook
and J. N. Maskleyne.
*(Keystone Press/British
Railways)*

of King's Cross each morning between 7.30 and 9.0 a.m. In order to allow passengers to remain asleep until a respectable time after the train had arrived — in some cases during the night — it had been the practice to group the sleeping cars together into trains and take out of the station the ordinary passenger stock, in order to release some of the platforms for the arrival of outer suburban trains. The ultimate train of sleepers might then consist of between 12 and 16 vehicles, generally of 450 — 600 tons in weight which, if the rail was greasy, would frequently cause the L1, with its high tractive power but low adhesive weight, to slip to a stand on the rising 1 in 105 gradient out of King's Cross through the Gas Works and Copenhagen Tunnels. Assistance then had to be given and this caused much delay to the morning services. But despite the severe start out of King's Cross Station it was not the practice to bank trains out. The speed restriction of 8 m.p.h. from several platforms through the throat area at King's Cross precluded the L1s from getting a good start at the gradient through the tunnels.

If the L1 succeeded in reaching Holloway it had another difficult gradient to surmount at Wood Green, where the Hertford Branch went over the top of the main line on a flyover with a short gradient of 1 in 51 and a sharp curve. In order to obtain the necessary impetus to get up the bank the driver would stop well back on the carriage road, then make a flying run round

Class A5 No. 69814 was transferred to King's Cross from Grantham to see if this heavy Great Central design would keep its feet better than the L1. It did but could not get up Wood Green bank with a heavy train as it was not powerful enough.
(P. N. Townend)

the back of Wood Green Station. This practice worked satisfactorily until the District Engineer enforced a 15 mph speed restriction on the back roads through Wood Green Station, whereas previously it had only existed at the south end of the station. This made things very difficult when rail conditions were adverse.

Much correspondence about the serious operating delays ensued from headquarters, which passed the blame down to the depot. In order to put the matter in its proper perspective some local practical tests were made, which involved trying the various types of locomotives available, including one of the last Great Central-designed A5s which was no longer required at Grantham. During the tests it was ascertained that the A5, despite its better adhesive ratio of 5.09, had insufficient tractive effort to lift 460 tons over Wood Green bank keeping to the 15 m.p.h. speed restriction at the foot of the gradient and slowly came to a stand without slipping or requiring to use the sands. In comparision an L1 in good condition was tried on a train of 490 tons and slipped to a stand twice with the steam sands still working; after the second slip it could not be restarted. The next locomotive tried was a New England B1, No. 61200, which unlike many of the King's Cross B1s was fitted with a combination of dry and steam sanding gear. This locomotive was the only one of the three classes tested to get over Wood Green bank, albeit at 4 mph and using the sands, but without slipping. Further B1s were tested and it was found that if fitted with dry sands there was a slight improvement over the L1: but if a slip occurred, the locomotive could not generally restart. As the rest of the day's work in the diagram required shunting to be carried out, the B1, being a tender engine, was not so convenient as the L1 tank.

The report concluded that if the work was to be done without causing delay some suitable tank engines would have to be transferred to Top Shed. After perusal of the dimensions of locomotives available at the time on British Railways, a formal request was made for some GWR 2-8-0Ts to be allocated. This silenced the complaints, but the locomotives requested did not materialise. So King's Cross carried on by using two L1's on the heaviest daily train, when the additional crew and locomotive were available, and using B1's on some of the other sleeper workings.

The L1s also had a tendency to become short-winded on a sharply-timed train first stop Welwyn Garden City. In order to improve punctuality and avoid embarrassment to some of the railway officers who travelled home each evening on the heaviest of these trains the 17.39 departure from King's Cross, which loaded to nine vehicles, became a regularly double-headed train. Usually a B1 was the leading locomotive, but the L1 was frequently bunker-first and the combination looked incongruous. The N2s had for many years almost invariably worked out of King's Cross chimney-first, but the practice never developed with the L1s, which generally worked either way round.

Right: The 17.39 from King's Cross, first stop Welwyn Garden City, was regularly double-headed as an L1 had a tendency to become short-winded on nine coaches. The train is seen passing New Southgate. (P. N. Townend)

Below: The L1s were used to work the heavy trains of sleeping cars out of King's Cross and would frequently slip to a stand between the tunnels or on Wood Green bank, when rail conditions were poor. No. 67800 is having no difficulty on a dry rail. (P. N. Townend)

9

Some Specials and Relief Trains

Over and above its diagrammed services, Top Shed depot was called upon to provide locomotives for many special workings, usually passenger but sometimes freight workings. Very often these were relief passenger trains worked in large numbers at holiday times, but over the years locomotives and crews were turned out for many important and occasionally unusual special trains.

The most important were the Royal Trains, generally run from King's Cross late at night, but nevertheless given locomotives turned out in exemplary condition. A standby pilot would be stationed at King's Cross Station and also, sometimes, at Hitchin, but the practice of running a light engine to "clear the line" ten minutes in front of the train had ceased many years previously.

Very careful inspections were made of the locomotives involved as well as checks in service. The coaling would be done by hand in the Repair Shop with the overhead crane, and specially selected grade 1A Yorkshire coal would be used. Externally the Royal locomotive was turned out immaculately with a white cab roof, polished buffers, motion, connecting rods, couplings, drawhooks and cylinder covers; if it was an A1 the smokebox door ring and hinges would be polished as well. If the locomotive was not ex-Works newly painted — and in many cases, when Chargeman Cleaner Dick Ball did not think it had been painted properly — it would be repainted locally by the King's Cross Painter, Frank Rayner, to whatever extent was deemed necessary. Rayner could paint a locomotive in a very short time, including retransfer of the numerals, BR emblems, letters and complete lining-out when required. When No. '61572, the last B12, was borrowed from Norwich for a special enthusiasts train in the closing years of steam it had been in store for some time and was not up to the usual standard of appearance on arrival at King's Cross. Three days later it worked its special train repainted and lined out; Frank had completed the red lines round the splashers as the engine was being oiled shortly before leaving the shed.

Right: Gresley and his two daughters stand alongside his latest locomotive No. 10000 in 1930 in the Milk Dock at King's Cross. (Express Photos Ltd)

Far right: North Eastern Class Z three-cylinder Atlantic No. 2210 waits on Top Shed for its return working. (I. Allan collection)

Bottom left: North Eastern Railway Raven Pacific leaving King's Cross during tests carried out soon after the railway amalgamation of 1923. The first NER locomotives, however, had worked into King's Cross in 1900 on troop specials. (Colling Turner Photos)

Not all Royal Trains were worked without incident, although none of the steam locomotives used failed in latter years. Perhaps the attempted coupling up of an A4 late one night at King's Cross came nearest to causing a delay. When the locomotive backed up to the LM Royal Train about a quarter-of-an-hour before departure time it was found that the buckeye coupling with which all LNER corridor tenders were fitted had jammed and would not engage properly. The locomotive could not be persuaded to move either way and an N2 had to be summoned quickly up to the front of the A4 to give it a good bump in order to release the buckeye. The emergency coupling was hurriedly attached and the "right away" given by the guard almost immediately. The driver put his cloth over the vacuum gauge and set off—but then it was realised that the tests laid down had not been carried out. An inquest held later at the depot ascertained that the LM Royal Train buckeye was higher than the standard laid down, whereas many couplings on the A4 tenders were set too low. The two buckeyes would not

match by several inches. In order to avoid recurrence of trouble it was made standard practice to send the locomotive booked to work the Royal Train out to Bounds Green Sidings specially to check it on the actual train before the latter left the sidings. In addition, the coupling height above rail level on all corridor tenders was regularly checked at the depot thereafter.

Later someone not employed by British Railways, when told of this, recalled that some years previously the A4s with corridor tenders had not been used on the Royal Trains from King's Cross; if necessary a non-corridor tender had been specially changed over from another locomotive at the depot. Whether this was anything to do with the fact that LMS vehicles were not fitted with buckeye couplings at that time I am unaware, but when the difficulty occurred about 1958 no one had any knowledge of such an instruction. A4s with corridor tenders were used regularly there-after; indeed, the corridor connection proved useful for leading the communication equipment through to the train.

On another Royal occasion a resplendent A1, No. 60157, was used. It was observed to leave King's Cross very steadily and enter the Gas Works Tunnel; but next morning we learned that it had come to a stand on the steep gradient just north of Gas Works Tunnel. The driver had taken things a little too slowly out of King's Cross. He had not gained enough speed to get up the gradient with the heavy LM Royal Train and had not realised this in the dark until he had come to a stand. No doubt he had taken it easily to avoid the risk of slipping, which could sometimes be a problem with the later, higher tractive-effort Pacifics under greasy rail conditions. However—and unusually in such circumstances—the driver had managed to restart without difficulty and got the train away without slipping so that no one was aware of the incident until later.

Gresley P2 Class *Mons Meg* leaving King's Cross in 1937. These locomotives rarely visited King's Cross and this working was probably for publicity purposes. *(Cecil J. Allen collection)*

There was an occasion in September 1961 when the depot was glad that it had turned out an A3 fit to work a Royal Train. The Royal Family had come by rail to Hitchin from Scotland for the funeral of the Lord Lieutenant of Hertfordshire at the family home of the Queen Mother at St. Pauls Waldenbury. King's Cross was required to work the empty stock back to Peterborough *en route* to Wolverton, where the LM Royal Train was normally kept. The Queen intended to fly back to Scotland immediately after the funeral, but at the very last moment, when the King's Cross A3 No. 60044 had actually left Hitchin with the empty stock, the flight was cancelled due to severe gales which caused considerable deforestation in the north of Scotland. The train was hurriedly brought back to Hitchin and the Royal Family returned north by train, the King's Cross A3 locomotive working through to Newcastle. This was the only occasion I knew of a Royal Train being provided at such short notice, with none of the usual circulars or even a booked path for it. The A3 had been turned out immaculately and in excellent mechanical condition by a chance decision—or was it intuition?—that it did not seem right to couple any old disreputable loco to such beautiful stock!

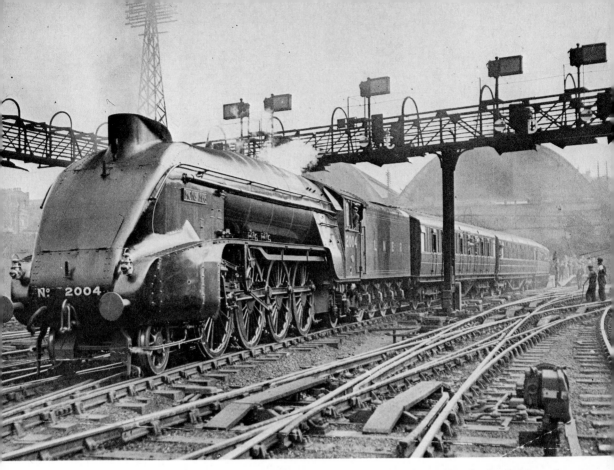

A number of special trains were laid on for the launching of ships in the North-East and for these special headboards were provided and painted locally at the depot. A suitable stock of blanks in three different shapes and sizes were held. Usually the depot would turn out whatever locomotive was convenient, frequently one recently seasoned after Works overhaul, but for the launch of the *Empress of Canada* on Tyneside the A4 locomotive *Dominion of Canada,* now preserved across the Atlantic, was requested for the special train from King's Cross to Newcastle which was to carry the High Commissioner of Canada and other dignitaries. This locomotive had been presented with a bell and a Canadian whistle before the war, but the bell had been removed to the Museum at York as there was no longer any room for it in front of the chimney after the locomotive had been fitted with a double blastpipe. The mileage run by the locomotive since its last Shops overhaul was approaching 90,000, but nevertheless the depot was instructed to turn the locomotive out like new. In five days the engine and tender were thoroughly examined, repaired, completely painted and lined out in the Repair Shop at Top Shed.

It was not unusual at bank holiday weekends and on peak summer Saturdays to diagram more trains to be worked by King's Cross Depot than the number of engines available. These trains

were always covered, however, and it was unknown to cancel a passenger train at such times. At these peak periods no locomotives were planned for boiler washout or preventative maintenance, but shopping of locomotives in Main Works generally continued although usually on a reduced scale for the Pacifics in the peak of the summer. It was the practice for a few days to borrow a large number of V2s from Doncaster, March and Peterborough, but many of these locomotives usually failed to benefit King's Cross for a variety of reasons best forgotten, as the V2 was basically an excellent locomotive for relief passenger trains. No other Region of British Railways, except perhaps the Southern, had a large-capacity locomotive available in such numbers to be called up for main-line passenger work when the need arose.

Any foreign engines booked to stand at King's Cross were used whilst the crews were in lodge, such as the Gateshead engine which came up overnight and returned next night at 10.15 p.m. on the "Night Scotsman". The Gateshead engine on this diagram frequently did a trip to Peterborough or Grantham when the need

Above right: Great Western King Class No. 6018 on arrival at King's Cross from Leeds on May 11th 1948. *(C. C. B. Herbert)*

arose. Similarly the Ardsley lodge turn V2 would be used in times of severe shortage of power, but care had to be taken to select the job for this engine after an Operating Enquiry had decided that the punctuality of the 1.20 p.m. train to Leeds had suffered as a consequence of the use on occasion of this depot's V2 locomotive. After all the Pacifics and Green Arrows had gone, Top Shed was down to B1s and the odd 9F. B1s worked regularly from King's Cross to Skegness on summer Saturdays and occasionally also to Grantham on an express, but King's Cross had only a small allocation of 4-6-0s and double-heading of these locomotives on the main line was rare, except occasionally with Immingham engines on a Cleethorpes train for operating reasons.

The most difficult period to cover on Saturdays in the peak months of the year was around 1.0 p.m. to 2.0 p.m. By this time every locomotive at Top Shed had gone out, but nothing was due to return until Train No. 971 Up arrived in King's Cross from Leeds at about 1.45 p.m. This brought back the locomotive which had gone down on the "Yorkshire Pullman" to Leeds the night

129

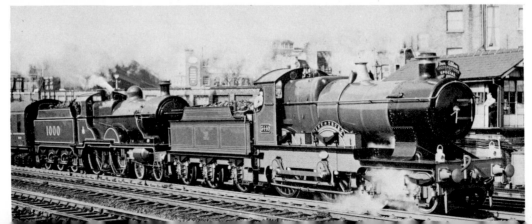

before. The engine concerned was not usually released to the depot until around 2.30 p.m., but on several Saturdays the 1.45 p.m. to Grantham required cover. On one occasion the depot was completely devoid of any tender locomotives except for a single 9F 2-10-0, which was turned out for the 1.45 p.m. The Down working presented no problem, as the train was light and stopped at a number of stations, but the return leg was on the "Heart of Midlothian" express.

The first time a 9F was used it was also known that the General Manager was returning on the Up train, so Grantham was duly requested to change the 9F for something more suitable. This was found to be impossible. It was surprise enough to see a 9F on such an important train, but still more astonishment was expressed when the King's Cross driver reached 93 m.p.h. down the bank from Stoke with it and made up time to London. On the following Monday criticism was voiced of the use of such an engine, despite the fact that it was a 9F or nothing. Eventually the circumstances were accepted, and then some effort was expended in trying to work out the maximum speed at which the locomotive should have been allowed to run. As no limit had ever been laid down previously for locomotives generally, except that prescribed by the overall 90 m.p.h. limit of the track, it was suggested by the Line Running Officer that the speed limit of the locomotive should be the number of inches the driving wheels were in diameter. This would, perhaps, have been fine for a 9F with 5 ft. 3 in. diameter wheels, which equalled 63 m.p.h. but when it was pointed out that Pacifics in future would have to be limited to 80 m.p.h. on this basis, no more was heard of a locomotive speed limitation.

The 9Fs continued with their very occasional Saturday express workings when the need arose, but one Bank Holiday Saturday not even a 9F was available. Control was asked to assist in finding a locomotive to cover the 1.45 p.m. from King's Cross, but replied that none could be found. Then, at 1.15 p.m., the Running Foreman was startled to see an A3 arrive on the turntable at the bottom of the yard. Everyone available was put on the locomotive to get it serviced quickly and within a few minutes it was *en route* to King's Cross to work the 1.45 p.m. A little while later Control enquired the whereabouts of the Pacific off a pigeon special which had arrived from Newcastle at Welwyn Garden City during the morning and which, as it could not be turned at Hitchin, had been sent up to Top Shed for turning. When told that the locomotive was already heading north from King's Cross on the 1.45 p.m., Control was not at all pleased; but the pigeon special saved the day and no difficulty was experienced in finding a King's Cross V2 later in the afternoon to work the empty pigeon boxes back to Newcastle.

In 1960 a series of special trains were worked to Doncaster for Ian Allan Ltd. The Midland Railway 4-4-0 compound locomotive No. 1000, preserved in beautiful condition at Derby, was borrowed and also *City of Truro*, the GWR 4-4-0, which was reputed to have attained 102 m.p.h. in 1904. The two locomotives

Class 9F No. 92196 with
express headlights passing
New Southgate on the
1.45 p.m. train to
Grantham. Class 9Fs were
occasionally used on this
train on Saturdays when no
other power was available.
(P. N. Townend)

ran double-headed from King's Cross to Doncaster and back, but unfortunately *City of Truro* failed at Peterborough on the return journey with a fractured cylinder oil pipe. This was only a small item to repair, but it gave the Midland compound the opportunity to work the train unassisted through to King's Cross.

The Midland locomotive was driven and fired by a Kentish Town crew, with a King's Cross pilot driver. Usually in steam days enginemen were expected to take any type of engine at sight without any additional training. Apart from the various interchange trials where the crew went with the locomotive, this was one of the few occasions when King's Cross men were not allowed to handle the engine, no doubt because the operation of the Deeley regulator, which worked the engine simple in the first position of the regulator handle, would mislead any driver not used to simple and compound working. However, a King's Cross main-line crew took *City of Truro,* the cab of which certainly presented them with a contrast to that of the more usual Pacific. This was the last occasion when 4-4-0s travelled the East Coast main line.

A few days later *Flying Scotsman,* No. 60103, was provided for another excursion for the same organisers, but this time from Marylebone to Doncaster. Not to be outshone by the other locomotives, No. 60103 was repainted and turned out with polished buffers, motion, and cylinder covers. It was ready a few days earlier and on a Bank Holiday afternoon given a run to Peterborough. At King's Cross it was seen by the Line Manager, who approached the driver and enquired, as the locomotive appeared so obviously fresh out of Works, whether it was sufficiently run in to work a main-line express. The driver declared that he knew nothing about that, but an Inspector who had been round the other side of the engine told the Line Manager that the engine had, in fact, run a considerable mileage since visiting Doncaster Works and had just been repainted locally. A few weeks later the Traffic Manager visited the depot. Mentioning the special trains worked recently, he remarked pointedly that the sponsors did not pay for the locomotive used to be painted.

On another occasion a B1 class 4-6-0, No. 61379 *Mayflower*, was borrowed from Immingham Depot, where it was allocated for much of its working life, for a Saturday morning excursion to Boston from King's Cross for an American Society from Boston, Mass. This locomotive had a particularly poor reputation for steaming and to crown things it arrived at King's Cross on a Friday evening with three driving axleboxes hot. It was impossible to lift the locomotive overnight, particularly as the wheeldrops were only manned on the day turn of duty. In addition, it could not have been run in again in the time available. A quick decision was therefore made to use a King's Cross B1, No. 61179, which could be easily renumbered 61379 for the occasion. New transfers were used on the cab side and the nameplates, number plate and commemorative plaques were all transferred from No. 61379. No one was any the wiser until a few weeks later a letter was passed to the depot for an explanation. It came from a small boy in the Birmingham area who asked, please Sir, could someone tell him why he had seen two engines with the number 61379 on King's Cross Shed on this particular Saturday morning? Confession being good for the soul, the truth was revealed and the depot was duly admonished and told not to do it again.

On Ascension Day in May 1959 a very odd little special train left No. 13 Platform King's Cross Suburban Station in the morning at 11.25, twenty-five minutes in front of the "Queen of Scots" Pullman and hauled by a J52. It was booked to haul an express train of two coaches, one the Traffic Manager's Saloon and the other a braked vehicle for the guard, and to run non-stop from King's Cross Station to some private sidings at Marshmoor. The

Below: No. 61379 *Mayflower* was sent to King's Cross to work a special train for an American Society to visit Boston, Lincs. As it arrived with three hot axleboxes No. 61179, a Top Shed B1, was substituted being renumbered and named for the occasion. *(P. N. Townend)*

locomotive was No. 68846, which had been acquired by Captain Smith for preservation. In order to hand over the engine in a dignified manner it had been decided to put it on the saloon and have lunch in the sidings. The two-coach special running on the main line just made it without delaying the following Pullman train, although it was touch and go for steam as it was difficult to fire the locomotive when running with four people crowded into such a small cab.

This J52 had been allocated to Hornsey for many years. When the Borough of Wood Green celebrated its 750th anniversary as a Chartered Borough, the railway decided to put on a Railway Exhibition at Noel Park station yard as their contribution to the festivities. At such events before the Second World War the LNER had gained considerable publicity from exhibiting new locomotives and rolling stock at many places from one end of the line to the other, but on this occasion King's Cross was given the task of providing the exhibits on a "do-it-yourself" basis. One of the last C12 4-4-2Ts was discovered at Grantham and brought up to London. This was a very suitable exhibit as these locomotives had worked King's Cross suburban trains for many years. A J52, No. 68846, was found at Hornsey underneath a thick layer of grime, and this was representative of a large number of Great Northern saddle-tanks which had been commonplace in the King's Cross area yards since the last century. *Mallard,* the world steam record holder, was provided by Top Shed and represented the LNER. A newly-built British Railways Class 9F, No. 92196, was borrowed from Doncaster and completed the steam exhibits.

All the locomotives were taken out of normal service and prepared locally to exhibition standards. No. 68846 certainly presented a challenge, as Hornsey had been at a low ebb for staff with which to clean steam locomotives for some years, but it was decided to repair the engine where it had visually deteriorated and repaint it completely. There was a desire to turn it out in green livery, but authority decided in accordance with the tradition of the London & North Western Railway that it did not matter what colour it was painted as long as it was black. This was done, but the painter was at least allowed to show his skill in the lining-out, which was the full British Railways standard of grey, white and red. On a J52 the cab panels and tanks were somewhat smaller than the BR locomotives more usually lined out, but the painter managed to get them all in. Certainly it was many years since a J52 had been seen by the public in such splendid condition. The steam exhibits were very popular at the Wood Green Exhibition and there was a lengthy and continuous queue to pass through the cab of *Mallard,* which was in steam. The most common question that everyone seemed to be asking was: what time train was *Mallard* going to work from King's Cross when the exhibition was over? A request was made afterwards for the J52 to be transferred to Top Shed, where it was used as Shed Pilot for some time. It is now preserved in Great Northern Railway livery as No. 1247 on the North Yorkshire Moors Railway.

Top: Class C12 No. 67352 and Class J52 No. 68846 were repainted and lined out for the Exhibition Commemorating the 750th Anniversary of the granting of a Charter to the Borough of Wood Green. The two locomotives stand in Noel Park Goods Yard. *(P. N. Townend)*

Centre: In May 1959 No. 68846 hauled a special express of two coaches out of Platform No. 13, King's Cross non-stop to Marshmoor where it was handed over to Captain W. G. Smith. *(P. N. Townend)*

Below: After the Wood Green Exhibition No. 68846 was used at Top Shed for shunting the shed. *(P. N. Townend)*

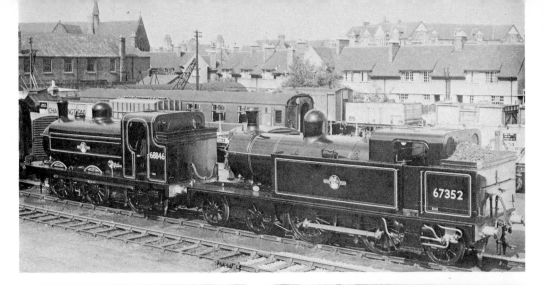

10

Living with the Pacifics

Top Shed was for many years associated particularly with the operation of the various types of Gresley Pacifics, and will always be remembered for the many notable performances achieved by King's Cross drivers with them. Although a number of the more modern Peppercorn A1 class were allocated to King's Cross for varying periods, representatives of the Gresley Pacifics were resident at Top Shed continuously for a period of over forty years, from their initial construction in 1922 until the depot closed in 1963.

The first authenticated 100 m.p.h. on rail in this country was attained by No. 4472 *Flying Scotsman* in 1934 with King's Cross Driver W. Sparshatt at the regulator during the course of a test run to Leeds and back. The train was a light one of only four coaches weighing 145 tons in the Down direction, and six coaches, weight 207 tons, on the return journey. Stoke summit was climbed at a minimum speed of 81 m.p.h. and Leeds reached in slightly under 152 minutes for the 185.8 miles. It was over 30 years before Leeds was reached more quickly than on this occasion.

The original Pacifics had, however, proved that they were fully capable of working much heavier passenger trains. In 1922 GNR No. 1471, whilst working from Top Shed, had successfully hauled, without assistance, a twenty-coach train of 610 tons in weight from King's Cross to Grantham and back in 121.5 minutes Down and 129.5 minutes Up for the 105.5 miles.

In the 1920s trains of over 500 tons in weight were commonplace on the East Coast Main Line, but speeds much in excess of 60-70 m.p.h. were not called for by the schedules of that time. Whilst the Gresley A1 class proved very successful in their haulage of these trains and eliminated much double-heading, their coal consumption tended to be somewhat heavy and the locomotives a little sluggish. Arising from the interchange trials of 1925, made in comparison with Great Western Railway "Castle" class locomotives, detailed alterations were made to the valve gear and higher pressure boilers fitted. This produced the A3 class, which were livelier and more economical engines.

King's Cross Driver A. Pibworth and Fireman E. Birkwood worked No. 4474 *Victor Wild* over the Great Western Railway main line from Paddington to Plymouth during the 1925 tests and Top Shed was host to No. 4079 *Pendennis Castle,* which ran between King's Cross, Grantham and Doncaster. In all, 51 of the 52 A1 class locomotives were eventually rebuilt to Class A3 over many years and 27 A3s were built new between 1928 and 1935. It became the practice to work the higher pressure locomotives on short cut-offs with full open regulator instead of the long cut-offs and partly open regulator used on the A1s in the 1920s, resulting in the achievement of better performances and a reduction in coal consumption.

A milestone achieved by the Pacifics in the summer of 1927 was the inauguration of non-stop engine workings over the 268 miles between King's Cross and Newcastle on the 9.50 a.m. relief to the "Flying Scotsman" on certain days of the week. The King's Cross crew lodged at Newcastle and returned the next day. This was the longest non-stop engine duty in the country at the time. It proved so successful that the following summer it was decided to run the 10.00 a.m. "Flying Scotsman" between King's Cross and Edinburgh in both directions non-stop over the 393 miles. Initially King's Cross crews shared the workings with Newcastle, but later Haymarket men participated and eventually replaced the Gateshead crews. King's Cross and Haymarket provided the locomotives on alternate days. This was the longest non-stop run in the world by far and attracted considerable publicity. A number of Pacifics had to be specially fitted with corridor tenders in order that the enginemen could change over *en route.*

The performances of the Pacifics during the 125 runs operated in each direction in 1928 were exemplary. Only one late arrival was recorded, due to a traction engine fouling the line on a level crossing at Chathill; and there was only one minor engine failure due to a defective mechanical lubricator, which caused the engine to be detached at Grantham, but King's Cross Driver Pibworth regained the 20 minutes lost and arrived in King's Cross 2 minutes early. The non-stop workings between King's Cross and Edinburgh continued during the summer months until the outbreak of war in 1939, but in 1937 the corridor tenders were

Flying Fox and *Pendennis Castle* at Top Shed in 1925. Arising from these trials higher pressure boilers were fitted and alterations to the valve gear made to the Gresley Pacifics. *(I. Allan collection)*

transferred to the A4s, which took over the workings from A3s.

In the spring of 1935, as a prelude to the regular operation of high-speed trains, a test train comprised of six coaches, weight 216 tons, was worked from King's Cross to Newcastle and back in the day by Top Shed A3 No. 2750 *Papyrus*. The regular driver, H. Gutteridge, took the engine in the Down direction and another well-known No. 1 Link driver, W. Sparshatt, brought it back from Newcastle. Both journeys were completed in under four hours and the average speed over the 536 miles there and back, allowing for checks, was just over 70 m.p.h. During the day 300 miles were covered at an average of 80 m.p.h. and on the return journey a maximum speed of 108 m.p.h. was attained between Little Bytham and Essendine, with an average of 100 m.p.h. maintained over 12 miles. The coal consumption throughout the day's work averaged just under 45 lb. per mile. No distance equal to this had ever been covered at such speeds previously.

Having proved that a high-speed train could be worked from King's Cross to Newcastle with steam traction in four hours, the LNER quickly put in hand construction of the "Silver Jubilee" train and four A4s at Doncaster Works. Six months later No. 2509 arrived at Top Shed and no other steam engine ever made a more spectacular debut than *Silver Link* on September 27 1935.

The new streamlined locomotive, which could hardly have been run in, took the new "Silver Jubilee" train on a publicity run with press and railway officials aboard from King's Cross to Grantham and back. Driver A. Taylor and Fireman J. Luty of Top Shed were the crew. A new record speed of 112½ m.p.h. was reached near Arlesey on the Down journey. Driver Taylor said after the run that as the speedometer was not working properly he was unaware of the speed he was attaining and was only restrained by Gresley himself, who came through the corridor tender to suggest that he should ease his arm as they had touched 112 mph twice and "there was an old Director in the back who was getting a bit touchy." The 25 miles between Mile Posts 30 and 55 were covered at an average speed of 107.5 m.p.h. and the 41 miles from Hatfield to Huntingdon at an average of 100.6 m.p.h. The total of 43 miles travelled continuously at an average of 100 m.p.h. has never been equalled since with British steam traction.

Three days later No. 2509 entered regular service with the "Silver Jubilee" and completed the first three weeks work in both directions on this train before No. 2510 became available at King's Cross. In the first 100,000 miles running, completed on July 2 1936, no time whatsoever had been booked against any A4s employed and over 18,283 miles had been run at speeds over 80 mph. Driver Taylor became somewhat of a national hero and was feted along with record holders in other spheres at the Trocadero Restaurant in London. He was later awarded the MBE and Gresley wrote to him personally in his own hand to congratulate him.

It is apparent that the Chief Mechanical Engineer, Sir Nigel Gresley, had considerable contact with his drivers and encouraged

them in their work, particularly at King's Cross. He was frequently seen meeting drivers and seeing them off on important occasions, and twenty years later it was rare to find a driver who would criticise an A4. This personal contact had existed from the very early days of the Great Northern Railway, but entirely disappeared after Gresley died. In the post-war era drivers became the responsibility of Locomotive Running Superintendents divorced from the Chief Mechanical Engineer's organisation.

With the success of the "Silver Jubilee" assured, the streamlined trains were increased in 1937 by the "Coronation" between King's Cross and Edinburgh and the "West Riding Limited" from King's Cross to Leeds and Bradford. The "Coronation" was undoubtedly the hardest of the trains to work. King's Cross shared the locomotive responsibility with Haymarket Depot, and King's Cross enginemen participated together with Gateshead and Haymarket crews. Edinburgh was reached in six hours, with a train weight of up to 312 tons in summertime when the beaver-tail observation saloon was attached. King's Cross also worked the "West Riding Limited" exclusively, providing both locomotives and crews.

Above: The two four o'clock expresses from King's Cross leaving Gas Works Tunnel. No. 4480 is applying sand to the rail. (G. R. Grigs)

Right: A silver A4 outside Doncaster Works receiving attention to the regulator valve. The handle for operating the "cods mouth" can be seen. The method of opening the front worked well but difficulty was experienced in keeping the handles available for use. (P. N. Townend)

One or two isolated cases occurred where the A4 working the "Coronation" train under adverse winter weather conditions ran short of coal at Hitchin. Tender coal capacity was therefore increased from a nominal 8 tons to 9 tons. In fact, it was later ascertained at Top Shed that over 11 tons could be stacked on by hand without becoming unsafe; after the war it was unknown for the "Elizabethan" to run short of coal, despite a much heavier though slightly slower-timed train. Generally there was sufficient coal left on the tender to work the engine another 100 miles.

Operation of all the streamlined trains was very successful from practically every point of view, except perhaps that of the Operating Department which had to keep the tracks clear for long periods; this created difficulties in pathing the slower-moving trains over some of the double-track-only sections. Morale was very high and the excellent publicity gained by the LNER was considerable.

By 1938 35 A4s had been built and, with the rebuilt W1, were also participating in the haulage of many of the LNER expresses from King's Cross to the north. The W1 was usually limited to travel between London and Doncaster due to track restrictions elsewhere, and was unusually fitted for a time with electric lighting, which illuminated the wheels when running.

The standard of performance and timekeeping on the East Coast main line generally in 1935-9 was never subsequently equalled with steam. Many feats of endurance were credited to individual locomotives working important turns over long periods. One was No. 4492 of Top Shed, which in 1937 worked the "Flying Scotsman" through to Edinburgh on forty-four consecutive days non-stop and eight further days with booked stops *en route* at weekends. A total of 20,436 miles were run in 52 days without need of anything but minor attention.

In 1938 Top Shed had an allocation of 11 A4s out of the 35 in

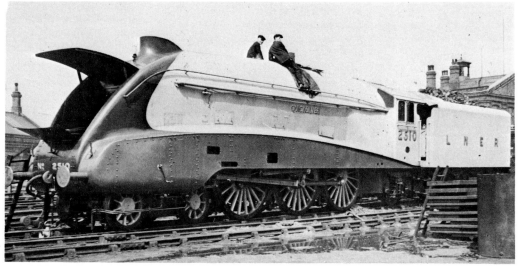

the class, but although the individual locomotives allocated varied somewhat, No. 2512, *Silver Fox* (later BR No. 60017) was at King's Cross from being built new in 1935 until the depot closed in 1963. This engine also achieved 113 m.p.h. near Essendine on the "Silver Jubilee" with the dynamometer car added in September 1936. This was a new record, and the only time it was achieved with a normal complement of fare-paying passengers on board the train.

Upon the outbreak of the Second World War a number of A4s at the principal depots, including King's Cross, were carefully stored away to await better days. After some months, however, all were restored to work on passenger trains which were heavier than ever worked previously over the LNER main line. The heaviest train recorded as hauled by an A4 was of 25 coaches, which weighed 750 tons tare and probably around 850 tons with passengers and luggage. Top Shed Locomotive No. 2509, *Silver Link* started this train from well inside Gas Works Tunnel and ran it through to Newcastle without assistance — and with a total time loss of only 15 minutes.

During the war, apart from losing their beautifully painted and maintained appearance as the locomotives were painted black, some minor alterations were made to the A4s. The side valancing, or skirting, which covered the motion was removed on all engines in 1941 to 1942 and never restored. This was done not only to give better access to the various parts of the valve gear but also to improve the air flow around the bearings, which before the war had already given trouble due to overheating. It was very doubtful if in practice it made any difference, as the change certainly did not prevent overheating of either the middle big end or driving axleboxes.

Commencing in 1943 all the Pacifics had part of the valve gear renewed in order to lengthen the maximum cut off from 65 to 75 per cent, thereby increasing the valve travel to $6\frac{5}{8}$ in. in full forward gear. Although this alteration was carried out in order to make the task of starting heavy wartime loads easier, it was not completed on all locomotives until the end of 1958.

Five A4 locomotives, including No. 60003 of Top Shed, were fitted with a middle cylinder reduced in diameter to 17 in. from the original dimension of $18\frac{1}{2}$ in. The intention was to reduce the load on the middle big end and so prevent failures. It was considered that the middle cylinder did more work then either of the outside cylinders due to imperfections in the Gresley two-to-one gear. The only Pacific locomotive indicated had been No. 2751 in 1931 and the cards taken then showed that up to about 60 m.p.h. and at maximum output the IHP was reasonably shared: but at higher speeds there was an imbalance with the centre cylinder producing more power. The modification was not perpetuated, but some of the modified locomotives remained so fitted for a number of years.

After the war the Pacifics were restored to their pre-war liveries for a time, until eventually, under British Railways, a dark

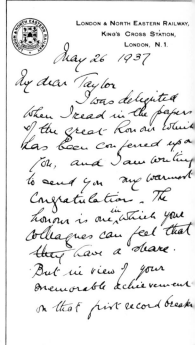

Above: The letter written by Gresley in his own hand to Driver Taylor congratulating him on being given the MBE. (*Mrs. G. Goddard*)

Above right: Sir Nigel Gresley and the 100th Pacific named after him pose outside the shed at King's Cross. (*British Railways*)

Right: Top Shed in Coronation Year with four of the Empire-named garter blue Class A4 Pacifics, and *Golden Eagle* on the far right painted green. (*Fox Photos*)

with the Silver
Lee, you have I feel
rightly deserved
..onour. You were
..irst to show what
..f my engines
.. really do.
..eel you have been
..ndated with letters
..ngratulation, and
..e though late is
..e the less sincere
..th kind regards
     yours sincerely
     A. Nigel Gresley

Brunswick green was standardised for all main-line passenger locomotives. A high-speed test run was made in May 1949 with *Silver Fox* exceeding 100 m.p.h. again, but none of the streamlined trains were restored.

In the summer of 1951 the non-stop working between London and Edinburgh was reintroduced with a train called "The Capitals Limited", which ran in front of the "Flying Scotsman", departing at 9.30 a.m. In the Coronation year of 1953 this train was renamed "The Elizabethan". The schedule was reduced to 6½ hours in 1954 but thereafter slightly eased.

King's Cross and Haymarket A4s and crews shared the working each summer and reliability and punctuality was of a high standard. Although the later A1s built from 1948 to 1949 were available, they could not be used on the non-stop as their tenders were not fitted with the corridors required to change the enginemen *en route* and the fitting of steam brake prevented an exchange of tenders with the vacuum-braked A4's.

About 1950, long-distance engine workings to Newcastle and Leeds were widely introduced on the East Coast route and the general level of all main-line services gradually accelerated. The through engine workings were soon reduced to a minimum again, however, because of poor engine performance. The former practice of changing engines at Peterborough, Grantham, Doncaster, York was restored until 1956 to 1957.

The position in 1956 was that all the original Gresley Pacifics had been rebuilt with 220 lb./sq.in. pressure boilers, 19 in. diameter cylinders, and together with the later locomotives thus built were classified A3. In the 1950's some A3 locomotives also received A4 boilers with the shorter tube length and combustion chamber, but the safety valves were set for an A3 at 220 lb./sq.in. The first the depot knew that A4 boilers were being used by Doncaster Works on A3s was when a set of superheater elements was ordered for A3 No. 60055 and it was found on fitting them that they were too long and projected through into the firebox.

What remained of an original Pacific locomotive by this time is somewhat conjectural. New bogies and main frames had been fitted at Doncaster Works during the course of normal repairs before the war and for many years it had been the Works practice to keep a Pacific chassis made up with cylinders ready for the next locomotive that required extensive frame repairs. This practice had not been confined to the A3s as No. 4455, one of the last C1s repaired, was given new frames, cylinders and boiler at its last repair before being withdrawn two or three years later. Over the years the A4s had, however, not given any trouble with main frames and apart from the normal renewal of components and the removal of the skirting over the wheels were basically as built.

In 1956 19 A4s and a few A3s were allocated to King's Cross. The depot was carrying out all its main-line work, express freight and the inner suburban passenger work wholly with Gresley-designed locomotives. Both the A3 and A4 classes were at a low ebb in performance and reliability, well below what had been

144

achieved when the locomotives had been new before the war. The reasons for this were varied and had proved difficult to identify and put right.

In the streamlined train era the A4s were new and were given very special maintenance, including main works overhaul at about nine-monthly intervals; rarely were they run over 60,000 miles before shopping. Added to this was the considerable pride of the engine crews and shed maintenance staff, as a result of the publicity gained by the LNER from the records achieved by the A4 locomotives. After many years of war and the period of austerity afterwards, there was difficulty in getting some aspects of locomotive servicing and maintenance performed satisfactorily. The Main Works shopping system was no longer based on priority for A4s; they had to take their turn with other locomotives when the Works could deal with them.

King's Cross received a high proportion of good coal, usually grade 1A or 2A for main-line work, but difficulty arose in segregating Welsh coal for suburban services and the smaller proportion of lower-graded hard coal, which was only suitable for short-distance work, as the coal hopper could only separate two sorts. King's Cross locomotives also received coal at depots where such a high proportion of grade 1A coal was not available. Some of the firemen on the main line were much younger and without the years of experience of some pre-war firemen; nevertheless, many of those in the top link were keen and enthusiastic.

Whilst numerous factors contributed to the general low level of availability and performance, the principal reasons were mechanical and inherent in the locomotives. The middle big end had always been a problem. It had overheated on pre-war occasions and on at least two of the high-speed record-breaking runs it had run hot. Similar trouble was also experienced during the interchange trials of 1948. Although a heat detector had been fitted inside the journal to give early warning of overheating, the skirting had been removed over the wheels and a few locomotives given a reduced middle cylinder of 17 in. diameter, little had been done to tackle the basic problem in the bearing itself. Overheated driving axleboxes had also occurred since the locomotives had been built and almost invariably it was the right driving which ran hot.

The most erratic feature of the locomotive's performance was, however, its steaming. Whilst results could usually be obtained by enthusiastic regular crews on their own locomotives, they were not achieved easily and poor timekeeping frequently resulted. King's Cross was, however, fortunate in having three double-blastpipe A4 locomotives with which anyone could get excellent results under the same adverse conditions afflicting the other locomotives. These three locomotives were used as far as possible wherever the best results were essential, such as on the "Elizabethan".

The middle big end on the various Gresley-designed three-cylinder locomotives was of a marine design and consisted of a semi-circular strap enclosing the brasses, which were fitted in two halves. At both the top and bottom of the strap were incorporated

large bolts, which were forged integrally with the strap and fastened through corresponding holes at the eye end of the connecting rod. The threads on the bolts were of knuckle thread. Between the butt ends of the strap and the connecting rod at both top and bottom were fitted brass gluts of the correct thickness. The two halves of the entire arrangement were held together by a large nut and a castle nut suitably cottered on each bolt. The brasses incorporated deep white metal pockets and the bearing surface was lubricated from an oil reservoir in the strap; the oil supply was regulated by means of a pin trimming which could be changed in size for running-in purposes.

The connecting and coupling rods of most of the Gresley three-cylinder locomotives had since 1920 been very light in weight, being manufactured from nickel chrome allow steel which gave the rods a characteristic ring. Weight compared to the more usual carbon steel was significantly reduced, to the order of 16 lb. per ft. for the nickel chrome connecting rod and 27 lb. per ft. for a carbon steel rod; the thickness of the web was exactly half. In 1936 the alloy steel was changed to include molybdenum. However, during the war the special steel was difficult to obtain and the general policy standardised since 1943 had been to substitute rods made of the more usual carbon steel. This decision was no doubt hastened by some serious failures of the alloy rods. Out of 60 which had failed and had been examined by the Metallurgist in the late 1940s, all but four were made of alloy steel; of this number, 40 were outside rods and no fewer than 34 were left-hand rods. Why such a large majority were from the left-hand side of the engine has never been explained. Most of the rods failed with fatigue fractures, but four failed with brittle fractures, including No. 2509 *Silver Link,* which broke both siderods on July 8 1943; the left-hand one splintered into 15 pieces and the right-hand rod was bent at right angles near the fork end.

From about 1937 a heat detector had been fitted inside a hollow in the middle crank pin. This was intended to give off a volatile liquid with a strong odour of peardrops—later changed to violets—if the bearing reached a temperature of 155 deg. F., thereby warning the driver before serious damage resulted. It was found that the smell persisted too long on occasions and caused drivers to fail locomotives after repairs had been carried out. The odour used was therefore again changed in 1948 to one that was less persistent, and aniseed became the standard. It was not always possible for the driver to detect the smell, however, and frequently considerable damage resulted to the crank axle journal and the cylinders before he became aware that anything was wrong.

It has been stated that middle big end failures were due to inequalities originating in the two-to-one gear, but this was not so. Failures of the middle big end were not confined to the Gresley Pacifics, but also occurred on all the other later varieties which were fitted with independent valve gear.

A different design of middle big end and connecting rod had been tried initially on one A4 in 1942 when Mr. E. Thompson became Chief Mechanical Engineer. Later a small number of the locomotives of the post-war A1 class were similarly fitted. This type resembled the design of the outside big end on a Great Northern Atlantic, insofar as the connecting rod was forked and the brasses were fitted into the fork. A glut was fitted behind the brasses and these were all held in position by a long bolt and cotter fitted through the strap and driven down tightly. Unfortunately the fitting on the A4 was not successful, as the cotter occasionally worked out with disastrous results; the fitting of this type of forked big end was not extended beyond the small number of locomotives treated experimentally.

Soon after 1950, a different type of brass bearing was adopted on both the Gresley and post-war Pacifics. The actual bearing surface consisted of a continuous, relatively thin white metal shell run on to a serrated brass surface, instead of the more usual brasses with much deeper white metal pockets. The bearing was bored accurately to a nine-thousands of an inch clearance over the journal diameter and to a high standard of finish. The gluts were changed from brass to steel and the lubrication was through a felt pad with no pin trimming. A fluted restrictor was fitted inside the oil reservoir in order to prevent the cork being pushed in too far, thus blocking the oil hole. Despite its name, it did not restrict the oil supply, which was regulated solely by the tightness of the felt pad. Success was not achieved until after it was realised that the felt pad had to be tightly fitted with a $\frac{1}{16}$ in. compression all round, and with the grain of the felt in the same direction as the oil flow. Special instructions were issued showing how this was to be done.

Considerable care was taken at Top Shed in carrying out this work, and also to ensure that the middle big end was properly examined at the 10-12,000 miles period laid down in the Schedule of Maintenance which was required on all locomotives on British

Railways. The mileage run by each locomotive was compiled by the Accountant from the drivers' daily bills and supplied to the depots as a four-weekly statement, but the statement was generally received some weeks after the end of each period. This was of no assistance in arranging 12,000 mileage examinations, as some Pacifics occasionally reached 10-11,000 miles in one four-weekly period. To ensure that the stipulated examination mileage was not exceeded, a careful daily record of mileage worked was maintained at the depot for each Pacific and V2 locomotive by a clerk called Horace Bussey, who had been a Boiler Foreman by profession and was now accommodated on clerical work for medical reasons. He was most meticulous in his work and every day the Shed Master was advised personally of any locomotive that had to be stopped in the next few days for examination.

It became an invariable rule that the mileage of 12,000 was not exceeded, and that the middle big end was taken down and properly examined, usually by Harry Billing, the Mechanical Foreman, and frequently by the Shed Master personally. If the white metal surface was in good condition and the journal clearance had not reached .020 in., the felt pad was renewed and the big end re-fitted for a further 12,000 miles. Generally it was found that no attention was required to the brasses at 12,000 miles, but nevertheless, whether any other item was done in the 12,000 miles examination or not, the middle big end was never missed.

After the bearing brasses had run 24,000 miles the white metal surface usually showed signs of deterioration. The brasses were then remetalled and accurately machined at the depot, although the instructions stipulated that they must be returned to Doncaster Works for this to be done. The machinist at Top Shed became very skilled in this work and achieved the high standard of accuracy and finish required. He had plenty of practice with the number of three-cylinder locomotives allocated to King's Cross.

A further precaution taken on the locomotive working the "Elizabethan" non-stop between Edinburgh and London daily in summertime was to check the amount of oil left in the reservoir when the locomotive came on shed. A little piece of paper would be left for the Shed Master each morning with "2¼ in." or possibly "1⅞ in." on it. This brief note was the assurance that the felt pad in the middle big end was still doing its job properly. The oil level would usually remain for weeks at about this figure, but as soon as the measurement fell to about 1 in. immediate action was essential the next time the locomotive returned from Edinburgh, or the reservoir would probably empty with consequent risk to the bearing. Much depended on the tightness of the felt pad; a belt-and-braces approach would have been preferable, by fitting a pin trimming to regulate the actual oil flow in addition to the felt pad, but the authorities could not be persuaded to accept this suggestion.

However, with attention to the detail described above, a middle big end failure on the King's Cross Pacifics and V2s was a very rare

148

occurrence by the end of the decade—in fact, the A4s on the "Elizabethan" duty of nearly 400 miles non-stop had no difficulty with the middle big end during the last few years the train ran. Perhaps the final vindication of this feature of the A4s was when No. 60007 achieved 112 m.p.h. for the Stephenson Locomotive Society on a Special train in May 1959, exceeding 100 m.p.h. three times during the day and ascending Stoke at a record minimum of 82 m.p.h. No. 60007 continued its normal working immediately after the run.

Removal of the valancing over the wheels of the A4s during the war afforded better access to the motion, but cannot be said to have helped to overcome the heated bearings experienced, as these continued unabated. There was so much draught around a locomotive in motion that it could not, and did not, make any difference.

Overheating of the right-hand driving axlebox on the Gresley Pacifics had occurred before the war, as was shown by the occasional failure and on the records at King's Cross, but with the regular shopping of these locomotives at Doncaster Works at lower mileages it had not been a serious problem. The nuisance became considerably worse when the Western Region method of optical alignment of the cylinders was adopted as standard workshop practice at Doncaster in the middle 1950s. Therafter the incidence of overheated right driving axleboxes rose to epidemic proportions on the A4s. In one particularly bad four-weekly period 11 of the 19 A4s allocated to King's Cross had hot boxes.

Up to this time a small number of standard axleboxes could be kept in the Depot Stores, and when required were bored out to suit the particular journal size and fitted to the locomotive. Under optical alignment any variations in the alignment of the main frames was counteracted by changes in the thickness of the axlebox flanges. Each driving axlebox became individual to the LH or RH position and standard axleboxes could not be used. This presented no difficulty with the later A1 class Pacific locomotives, as the axleboxes ran from shops and did not require changing at depots; but with a large fleet of A3s and A4s to keep running, it became a serious problem. Each axlebox required had to be ordered specially from Doncaster, where it was machined to the last recorded alignment dimensions, then supplied to the depot for fitting. This usually took three or four weeks and clearly something had to be done.

Initial representations to Doncaster produced the reply that as no casualty reports had been received the problem did not exist. These casualty reports had to be submitted by depots for delays of five minutes to passenger trains and ten minutes for freight trains, or if the locomotive failed to complete its working, also in the case of certain defined serious failures such as fractured axles. If heated bearings were found after completion of a working, they were not strictly considered casualties; and as depots were judged on how few casualties appeared in the league tables, casualty reports, whilst intended to reveal weaknesses, did not necessarily reflect the true situation. It was, however, in the interests of the depot to see that casualty reports were submitted for such items thereafter and King's Cross became a little unpopular with the other depots further north for revealing their failures too.

Having put the paperwork right, the Works increased the clearances when optically aligning the A4s and the epidemic subsided to the previous level, which was still too many in view of the increasingly higher mileages required between classified repairs. In order that King's Cross could deal with hot boxes more quickly and as standard axleboxes could not be fitted, it was agreed that a spare pair of driving axleboxes would be supplied to King's Cross Depot, machined to the optical alignment dimensions and stamped with the locomotive number and position on each occasion a locomotive returned from General repair at Doncaster Works. The Stores at King's Cross at one time held 38 individual axleboxes in stock for the 19 A4s allocated at that time (fortunately no one worried unduly about the value of the stock held). Some time later, after one of the A4s had returned to Doncaster for overhaul, the Works complained that a right-hand axlebox had been fitted to the left driving position and the left in the right driving position. It emerged that Top Shed had a left-handed fitter who had put them in the wrong way round, but as the locomotive had run a considerable mileage in this condition without anyone knowing it dented the case for optical alignment.

As there was usually no obvious external reason for the hot right driving axleboxes that continued to occur, it was decided to carry out a local investigation to see if the problem could be overcome. By examination of the driving axleboxes at different mileages, it was ascertained that the wear in the crown of the axlebox was of the order of ¼ in. to ⁵⁄₁₆ in. at a mileage of 40,000 at the inside end of the bearing. This caused the white metal crown to break up and most failures were found to occur at mileages of over 40,000. The wear at the outside end of the bearing was usually small, but the wear on the right-hand side axlebox was always slightly greater than that of the left-hand axlebox.

The No. 6 mileage examination, carried out at intervals of 36,000 miles, required the valves and pistons to be removed, cleaned and new rings to be fitted, the connecting and coupling rods to be taken down and examined, and the bushes and pins to be renewed as necessary. It was also the practice at Top Shed to take down the Gresley two-to-one valve gear at the same time to check and renew any pins and bushes found worn. With the rods down, the opportunity arose and was now taken to renew the driving axleboxes. This was carried out at King's Cross as a standard practice and the problem of overheated axleboxes in service was completely overcome.

The cause of the right driving axlebox wearing excessively at one end of the bearing in this taperwise fashion was not proved, but it was probably due to the three cylinders driving on the one axle, which made it difficult to brace the frames adequately as a structure immediately in front of the crank axle. All the post-war

Pacifics had divided drive and were free of this particular axlebox trouble. When the driving axleboxes were removed, one could sometimes see that the main frame was bent slightly inwards at the bottom corner of the horns; it would appear that the frames flexed slightly in service. The main frames on the A4s rarely gave any trouble with fractures, although many of the A3s had to be fitted with new three-quarter frames. No A4 had the cylinders indicated to ascertain the power output of each cylinder and on each stroke, but the results of the tests with A3 No. 2751 *Humorist* in 1931 mentioned previously also showed a tendency for the RH cylinder to do a little more work than the LH side, which might be the reason why the right driving axlebox suffered a slightly greater wear than the left axlebox. With the benefit of hindsight the fitting of roller bearing axleboxes to the A4s would probably have been justified and might have overcome the difficulties with the axleboxes in the long term. Three King's Cross A4 engines did have roller bearings fitted to the tenders and they gave excellent service for over twenty years before one or two bearings had to be replaced.

When the number of Pacifics concentrated at King's Cross had reached 42 in the autumn of 1957, the work required to maintain them was difficult to complete. Fitting staff were hard to recruit in the London area. At the same time many components were sent to Doncaster for repair at the 36,000 mileage examination, while the driving axleboxes had to be despatched from Doncaster to King's Cross to be fitted. It was therefore decided that it would be easier all round if the Top Shed A3s and A4s were sent to Doncaster for the No. 6 mileage examination to be carried out there. The Plant Works had never previously been required to carry out running shed examinations and some locomotives were dealt with before it was discovered that the staff concerned had never seen a copy of the requisite maintenance schedule. This was quickly put right and excellent co-operation was achieved with the Works. The practice of carrying out this work at Doncaster continued to the end of steam at King's Cross, and helped considerably in achieving very high mileages between General repairs.

The one alteration in detail to the A3s and A4s which made the most remarkable improvement in performance and reliability was without a doubt the fitting of all locomotives in both classes with the Kylchap double exhaust system. Four A4s had been built with the fitting when new in 1938 after successful trials had been carried out on A3 No. 2751 *Humorist*. King's Cross were allocated three of the A4s so equipped in 1948 and these locomotives had always been better performers than others in the same class. In the prevailing conditions of the 1950s this difference had become more marked. Gresley was indebted for the fitting to Monsieur Chapelon of the French Railways and Chapelon had checked the details before the arrangement had been first fitted to the P2 class in 1934. It was also known from calculations made by Gresley's staff that the reason why *Mallard* had touched 126 m.p.h. and greatly exceeded the 108-113 speed range reached by several different locomotives under high-speed tests was due principally to this fitting.

The Kylchap double blastpipe enabled the locomotives to steam very much more freely and without the skill and attention essential on the single-chimney locomotives. Perhaps even more important, there was a considerable reduction in back pressure due to the very large increase in the cross-sectional area of the blastpipe orifices, which allowed the engine to run more freely and obtained some increase in the effective power of the locomotive.

On the single chimney Pacific engines the diameter of the blastpipe top varied between 5 in. and 5¾ in. diameter over the years, depending on the type of top actually fitted; this compared with two orifices of 5 in. diameter in the Kylchap system applied to the Pacifics. The plain double blastpipes fitted to the *Duke of Gloucester* and LM Pacifics were each 4½ in. in diameter and on the "Castle" class 3⅞ in.

Gresley had stated in 1934, referring to the fitting of the slightly larger Kylchap double blastpipes to the P2 class, that in consequence the back pressure on the pistons was reduced from 7 or 8 lb./sq.in. to only about 2 lb./sq.in. when running at speed. It had also been intended to continue the fitting of the Kylchap system to any further locomotives constructed and the drawing office was suitably advised to do so, but it is apparent that no one was instructed to alter the locomotives already in service, possibly with an eye on the expiry of the patent rights due in 1941.

The war followed quickly the record-breaking run of *Mallard* in 1938 and the next locomotives to be fitted were the various rebuilds by Edward Thompson — No. 2005 from Class P2 which had been the only P2 with a single blastpipe, No. 4470 from the original Gresley A1 Pacific, No. 3696 of Class A2/1 and others which followed.

Gresley had experimented with different sizes of single blastpipe tops on the earlier Pacifics in an attempt to find a diameter that would enable the locomotive to steam and yet not unduly restrict it when working hard. No. 4472 on its record exploit in 1934, when 100 m.p.h. was attained, had been fitted with an altered top to enable it to run more freely.

The single chimney A4s had been built with a Churchward jumper top arrangement used on GWR locomotives, which allowed steam to escape through an annular ring around the top when the top lifted as a result of the engine working hard. This fitting had caused difficulty insofar as it became carboned up and required frequent cleaning to keep it movable and central to the chimney. King's Cross had bolted most of these down to the minimum diameter position of 5³⁄₁₆ in. in an effort to improve the steaming of the A4 locomotives, but many were removed altogether at the depot and a variety of blastpipe tops with different heights and diameters tried.

The Chief Mechanical and Electrical Engineer had also been approached with a request to improve the situation. So the

Class A4 No. 60033 *Seagull* is waiting to leave shed for "The Scarborough Flyer", which was worked on certain days during the week in summer only.
(P. N. Townend)

152

decision was made in 1953 to alter experimentally the design of the smokebox proportions on some A3s and A4s to Western Region dimensions. When the Drawing Office at Doncaster asked what these proportions were, a sketch was provided of the empirical ratios which had been found satisfactory on a Dean 0-6-0 about 50 years previously and no doubt used as a standard by Swindon since! The locomotives fitted with these ratios made a magnificent noise, but they were sluggish when being worked hard up some of the long 1 in 200 gradients on the GN main line. When the Chief Mechanical and Electrical Engineer was advised that the A4s altered to Western Region proportions were really no better and all that was required was to fit the other locomotives with Kylchap double blastpipes, which had always steamed and run freely, the reply was to fit some more locomotives with altered Western Region proportions.

In the meantime, the depot at King's Cross continued with its own tests with the single blastpipe caps, one of which was just a hole in a thick flat plate bolted to the top of the blastpipe. Difficulty was caused, however, when one of these altered engines arrived in Works and, of course, the Works refitted the standard jumper top arrangement before the locomotive was returned to traffic. Enquiries were made locally as to why the single-chimney A4 locomotives had not been altered to double blastpipes and it was suggested by the district office that they would need a new middle cylinder casting. In order to ascertain if there was any truth in this assertion, the "X" Day Chargehand Fitter, Arthur Taylor, was asked to go on two A4 locomotives, one of each type, in the shed, measure up everything in the two smokeboxes and report at the end of the day exactly what was required to change the single blastpipe locomotive to the double. When Arthur came back, his cryptic conclusion was: "Undo four nuts and make a bigger hole in the top of the smokebox and you are there".

Further advice offered at this time was that it was not desirable "to have all that gear inside the smokebox"; this was a reference to the series of cowls fitted between the double blastpipe tops and the chimney, which made it impossible to get at the tubes to clean them out. If this was so and as it had been very rare to take the cowls out for any reason at King's Cross, one could only conclude that no one had cleaned the middle tubes out at depots on those engines fitted for nearly 20 years! Nevertheless, a method of blowing the tubes out from inside the firebox with a compressed air gun was devised in order to overcome this objection. The fitting of the cowls between the blastpipe and chimney was an essential feature of the Kylchap exhaust system as it enabled a larger diameter blastpipe to be fitted and thereby further reduced back pressure; also a more even pull on the fire across the tubeplate was exerted. An enquiry from the BRB at about this time asked if it was correct the Kylchap-fitted locomotives did not steam properly: did the depot want the Kylchap double blastpipes removed? The reply made it clear that all that was required was alteration of all the other Pacifics, as the Kylchap-fitted

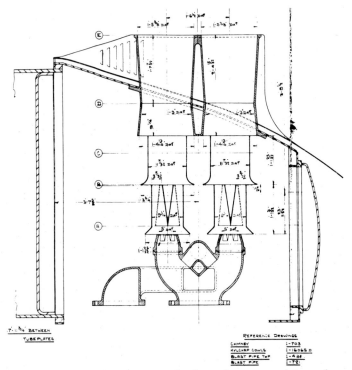

locomotives steamed and ran perfectly and were much superior to those with the standard arrangement.

As none of the various approaches made seemed likely to bear fruit, it was decided to tackle the problem of getting the Pacifics altered on the different basis of economy and money saved. The interchange trials in 1948, in which the three King's Cross double blastpipe locomotives participated, had shown that the double-chimney A4s used throughout the exchanges were more economical on coal used per drawbar horse power produced than any other equivalent locomotive tested. No. 4901 had also produced remarkably low coal figures when working from Gateshead in 1939. Comparative tests were therefore instituted by Top Shed using single and double blastpipe locomotives on the 8.20 a.m. King's Cross to Doncaster round working for five days each. The coal was weighed on and off with the overhead crane in the Repair Shop, thereby obtaining an accurate assessment of the coal used on each round trip.

The two locomotives used were of similar mileage since Main Works overhaul, but initially the results were inconclusive as the double-blastpipe locomotive romped away with the train, easily arriving before time and recovering any time lost due to other causes, whereas the single-chimney A4 had difficulty in keeping the point-to-point times and required the recovery margin shown in the timetable to arrive on time. It was decided therefore to repeat the tests with the double-blastpipe locomotive, this time curbing the driver's enthusiasm, also instructing the Inspector to

Above left, right: The interior of the smokebox of the Class A4 with the single chimney and with the Kylchap double chimney. The blast pipe orifice was originally $5\frac{3}{16}$ in. in diameter and the two Kylchap orifices were each 5 in. in diameter. *(British Railways/Science Museum)*

154

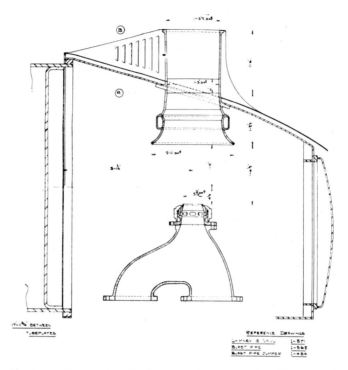

maintain strict sectional times and to use the freer-running characteristic of the locomotive to close the regulator and coast at every opportunity. Not having use of a dynamometer car to measure the coal used in relation to the power produced, this was the best that could be done locally by the depot.

The results were now conclusive and showed a saving of about 7 lb. of coal per mile in favour of the Kylchap A4. Depots at this time had an organisational line to the General Manager and it was used to advantage on this occasion to obtain authority for all the A4s to be converted on the basis of the coal saved. The cost of the modification was just over £200 for each locomotive and all the A4 locomotives were quickly converted between May 1957 and November 1958. This fitting removed the black sheep from the class and the excellent performance of the locomotives originally fitted became standard for the remainder.

The maintenance records at Top Shed were checked for some time after fitting. No A4 locomotive had been short of steam and none had required the smokebox joints testing with water to try and find any steam leaks that might have destroyed the smokebox vacuum. This had been a frequent occurrence previously and had probably caused more joints to leak. Most curiously, however, drivers completely omitted to book valves to reset, as they could no longer hear any irregularity in beat due to the very soft exhaust with the Kylchap system.

After authority had been given to fit the A4s with Kylchap double blastpipes, trials were quickly carried out locally in order

to justify treatment of the A3s on a similar basis of fuel saved. The savings in coal came out at a little less with an A3 compared to an A4 of around 6 lb. per mile locomotive: but the cost of conversion was also less, at £153, because there was no streamlined front to alter. King's Cross locomotive No. 60055 was the first to be altered, in June 1958, and the remainder of the class were modified before the end of 1959.

The A3s particularly were given a new lease of life. Whereas it had been the practice to keep these locomotives off the most arduous turns to Newcastle whenever possible in preference to the more powerful Class 8 Pacifics of Class A1 and A4, the A3s once again handled any of the main-line expresses from King's Cross to Newcastle and Leeds, and were frequently used on the tightly-timed "Talisman" and "Tees-Tyne Pullman" trains.

The first Class A3 fitted with a Kylchap double blast pipe in 1958 at King's Cross near the turntable. *(British Railways)*

In 1958, when only one King's Cross A3 had been converted, No. 60059 was called into Doncaster Works for a few days to be fitted with the automatic warning system. It had run nearly 70,000 miles since overhaul but was not on very arduous work. Doncaster Works was persuaded specially to fit the locomotive with a Kylchap double blastpipe whilst it was in Works for the automatic warning system to be fitted. It came back to Top Shed and was booked out on the "Yorkshire Pullman" to Leeds. The driver commented on his return that it was a beautiful locomotive now that it had been given a General repair—in fact it had not been touched mechanically at all!

Fitting the double blastpipes to the A3s brought up the old problem of smoke deflection again. Drivers complained that with the much softer exhaust the smoke and steam beat down, obliterating their view of signals from the cab. This was particularly so under easy steaming conditions, and on some days when there was a crosswind the driver's vision was completely cut off for long distances down the main line. A request was therefore made for smoke deflectors to be fitted and the next four A3s through Doncaster Works were fitted experimentally with small deflectors on top of the smokebox. Two of these were at King's Cross and under the experimental procedure depots were requested to report periodically on the results achieved. No. 2751 *Humorist,* had been similarly fitted in 1937 after encountering the same problem following the fitting of the double chimney, but this type of deflector was later discarded. The results of the various tests on smoke deflection had been published before the war and it was strange that Doncaster went back to this fitting 20 years later.

A report was therefore submitted that the small deflectors were not particularly effective, and that the pre-war tests had shown no form of deflection tried had been successful except the stream-lined front end of the A4s, which was hardly likely to be fitted to the A3s at this late stage. Doncaster was urged to try the Deutsche Bundesbahn type of deflector, and a side view photograph of a DB 01 class Pacific taken a few months earlier in Cologne was submitted with the information that the German Railways obviously had faith in this type of deflector as many locomotives

156

had been converted to it from the more usual type. It was requested that a King's Cross locomotive should be fitted so that it could be tested in service. A few weeks later a drawing was received and the fitting of four locomotives authorised.

The first A3 thus modified at Doncaster Works was a Grantham locomotive, No. 60049, but as soon as it was known that it was out of the Works arrangements were made for the locomotive to be loaned to King's Cross for tests. It was run to Newcastle and back on the diesel diagram, 10.00 a.m. ex King's Cross returning on the 5.5 p.m. from Newcastle, a round working of 536 miles in just over 12 hours. Several trips were made with different Inspectors timing how long the driver's vision was obliterated and the total time in over a week's running came to 25 seconds. The locomotive was also observed from the lineside, at different places and the exhaust was seen to lift clear of the cab even passing under a signal gantry. It was also checked at Knebworth and of three consecutive passing trains, one with a 9F, another with a Class A1 and on the third No. 60049, the A3 was the only one that completely lifted the smoke from the whole train. The 9F carried a pall of smoke in front of the chimney, and on both the A1 and 9F fitted with full size deflectors the exhaust steam drifted down by the cab and tender. These German deflectors completely overcame the problem and also had the advantage of not obstructing the running plate or the front of the engine. There was, therefore, no hesitation in recommending these deflectors for the remainder of the A3s on the grounds of safety. In order that the Top Shed locomotives should be fitted quickly, Doncaster Works were asked to send several sets of the deflectors to King's Cross and a number of locomotives were equipped at the depot.

Whilst some enthusiasts may have felt that the appearance of the A3s had been ruined by the so-called "elephants ears", it was an essential fitting with the Kylchap exhaust system. As the performance of the A3s had been so greatly improved, it has been stated that they were rebuilt; but only these very minor alterations mentioned above were necessary to bring both the A3s and A4s to this peak of performance.

After the A3s and A4s had been dealt with, efforts were made to have the V2s altered. King's Cross had an allocation of about a dozen of these locomotives for the important and heavy express freight trains from King's Cross Goods to Doncaster and York, but at holiday times and during the summer the V2s were frequently used on main-line express work.

The V2s were excellent locomotives basically, but many did lose time on the main line due to indifferent performance, particularly when suddenly called upon to work the faster passenger trains.

For some years the V2s had been shopped at Darlington and King's Cross found it necessary to reset the valves on every locomotive received back from this Works; this was rarely, if ever, necessary on a locomotive after being shopped at Doncaster. A prolonged argument ensued. Darlington claimed that the valves were set exactly in accordance with the valve event tables produced by Doncaster Drawing Office, and Doncaster Works said they followed the same tables. Nevertheless, the V2 locomotives were not set correctly. The answer eventually emerged that Darlington made no expansion allowance for the valves being set cold, whereas Doncaster did. To satisfy all concerned the drawing was suitably amended and the point clarified. After some further difficulty through getting the expansion allowance for the middle valve the wrong way round, the V2s after many years of construction and maintenance at Darlington, were finally set correctly by the 1960s.

Comparative coal consumption tests were made with a V2 on the 8.20 a.m. King's Cross to Doncaster working in order to justify the fitting of the Kylchap exhaust system. But, as many of the Top Shed firemen knew, a good V2 was more economical on coal than some of the Pacifics. Purely on a coal consumption basis on this particular working, the V2 came out at around 41 lb. per mile compared to about 45 lb. per mile for the double blastpipe A3 and A4, but this was not properly related to the power output produced and timekeeping was not strictly observed. A case could not be made out on the basis of economy. After some delay it was eventually agreed that two V2s would be fitted with double blastpipes, but this time the BRB insisted on BR design.

A Doncaster V2 locomotive, No. 60817, was one that was fitted, but under test it was found to perform about the same as a good V2 with single chimney. The plain double blastpipe fitted did not have the Kylchap arrangement of cowls and had the smaller blastpipe orifices of $4\frac{1}{2}$ in. diameter. Although time was running out for steam traction on the main line, authority was finally given to fit six locomotives with the Kylchap double exhaust system on the strength of having to cover any diesels which failed at Peterborough and particularly the Deltics. A standing pilot was always kept at Peterborough Station and the pilot could not be bigger than a V2 as the turntable at the station would not turn a longer engine. One or two double blastpipe V2s were certainly kept at Peterborough for this purpose, but several of the other V2s fitted were usefully employed from Top Shed on the express freight trains to York.

The "Anglo-Scottish Car Carrier" leaving King's Cross Goods Yard on its inaugural run. Class A4 No. 60032 *Gannet* is fitted with Kylchap double blast pipe. *(P. N. Townend)*

ANGLO-SCOTTISH
CAR CARRIER

60032

The fitting of the Kylchap double blastpipe again made a remarkable improvement to the V2s. Complaints about late running of the 4.5 p.m. King's Cross Goods to Dringhouses, which had been common for some time, disappeared overnight. No. 60881 was used soon after fitting on a passenger train into King's Cross and the Doncaster Inspector riding on the locomotive reported that the locomotive was transformed: he had to instruct the driver to close the regulator at 95 m.p.h. in order to prevent the locomotive exceeding 100 m.p.h. One of the enginemen's representatives at New England was also heard to say that it was not diesels they wanted but Kylchap double blastpipes! Whilst the fitting justified its cost by the improved performance given in the short time the locomotives were fitted, the V2s now had only a short life ahead of them. In fact, these were the last improvements made to any of the King's Cross locomotives.

Little mention has been made so far of the Gresley two-to-one valve gear fitted to all his three-cylinder locomotives, and for a simple reason: despite its unpopularity, which became fashionable after Gresley died, the gear did not present any special problems. A failure of a component of the two-to-one valve gear on the road was virtually unknown, though one cannot say the same of the middle eccentric, which occasionally did cause serious failures. Certainly it could not be said that the performance of the engine was affected by using conjugated valve gear, as no other class exceeded the records produced by the A4s; the problem of the middle big end was resolved without any reference to it.

From the shed point of view, the real difference between the Gresley valve gear and the independent valve gear fitted to the later Pacifics was that the Gresley system was grease lubricated and did not require daily attention. The independent valve gear incorporated a middle eccentric, the reliability of which was dependent upon the driver filling the reservoir with oil on every trip and replacing the cork tightly; it was difficult to get at the middle eccentric, and it is little wonder that occasionally the oiling was missed or the cork not replaced properly. There was therefore a distinct advantage in eliminating this feature.

The A1 class was the last LNER Pacific design and its 49 locomotives had been built after Nationalisation in 1948 to 1949. Some went new to King's Cross, but a concentration of locomotive types had resulted, after a short time, in the King's Cross A1s being transferred away to Grantham and Copley Hill. In return all 19 A4s in the Eastern Region had been placed at King's Cross, together with a small number of A3s. But in 1956 to 1957 through engine workings to Newcastle and Leeds were reintroduced and 12 A1s returned to King's Cross.

The A1 differed from the A4 in having divided drive and three sets of Walschaerts valve gear. The grate area was increased to 50 sq.ft. and the cylinders enlarged to 19 in. diameter. The A1s were the culmination of 25 years' practice in the designing of Pacifics at Doncaster and from the railway's operating point of view they were most successful locomotives. This was apparent in

Below: Class A3 No. 60049 *Galtee More* was the first fitted with the German type smoke deflectors and was tested on "The Flying Scotsman" diesel diagram to Newcastle, the return journey being completed in a few minutes over twelve hours. These smoke deflectors were very satisfactory. *(P. N. Townend)*

Above: Class A3 No. 60055 *Woolwinder* leaving King's Cross on the "Yorkshire Pullman" when fitted with the small deflectors, which were of little value. *(P. N. Townend)*

their consistent reliability, economy in operation and the high mileages run daily. Depots appreciated that the locomotives required less maintenance and this was reflected in the repair costs per mile for an A1, which totalled 8.53 pence compared with, for example, 12.70 pence for an LM "Duchess". Although figures on their own can be misleading the A1 was by far the cheapest Class 8 engine to maintain on British Railways and approximated in this respect to some of the much smaller two-cylinder BR 4-6-0s.

The standard A1 gave no trouble with heated driving axleboxes, but five locomotives had been fitted with an experimental design of split axleboxes to the driving wheels. Although not allocated to King's Cross at the time, this quintet caused such exasperation by their frequent arrivals at King's Cross with one or more axleboxes hot that Top Shed put forward and obtained authority for Doncaster Works to convert them back to the more usual axlebox arrangement. The A1's middle big end caused similar trouble to that of the A4, but this was overcome in the 1950s by carrying out the same detailed alterations to the brasses and gluts.

Five A1s had been fitted when new with roller bearings to all axleboxes on the engine and tender. Two of these locomotives, Nos. 60156 *Great Central* and 60157 *Great Eastern,* came to King's Cross in 1956 and probably ran consistently the highest mileages of any locomotive King's Cross had ever had. As stated earlier, one of them covered 197,000 miles before going to Doncaster for a Heavy repair and the other reached 96,000 miles in twelve months' normal service.

Comparing the mileages of the twelve A1s allocated over a period of six months to that run by the 19 A4s, each A1 averaged 6,400 miles per four-weekly period and each A4 4,800 miles per locomotive. The difference was due to the A1's need of less time on depot and works for repairs and maintenance. The first A1 was said by Mr. J. F. Harrison, in his presidential address to the Institution of Locomotive Engineers, to have reached a million miles in twelve years, which represented an average of 236 miles every day. Whilst it was a roller bearing A1 that was the first to reach the million miles, the average miles per day for the whole class, was 216; by comparison the first A4s were only approaching 1½ million miles after 25 years' service. Unlike some similar records of the past, no special arrangements had been made to achieve these results; it is doubtful if any other high-capacity express locomotives in this country have ever approached this standard for a whole class.

Nevertheless some maintenance problems did arise with the A1s. Strangely, these were entirely different to those of the other Pacific locomotives at King's Cross. Perhaps the oddest item developed from the complaint of a Member of Parliament that he had observed a King's Cross A1 arrive at Newcastle with a row of bolts loose and broken, lying on the footplate at the front of the locomotive. These bolts had fallen from the smokebox cradle and it had been found very difficult to keep them tight on certain A1

locomotives; on other engines the smokebox rivets worked loose at the joint which held the smokebox to the front ring of the boiler. The boiler expansion arrangements were probably the root cause of the difficulty, for the A1s differed from the Gresley designs in having a small additional saddle under the front ring of the boiler which rested on a stretcher between the frames. Initially this had a flange on either side, which could possibly restrict the expansion of the boiler, but one of the flanges was eventually removed. Also the smokebox was also strengthened by an extra thickness of plate for both the smokebox saddle and the smokebox riveted joint to the boiler. These alterations improved the situation.

From the enginemen's point of view the A1 locomotives could pull anything put to them and the only complaint concerned their riding. There was no vibration or hardness as experienced on the "Britannia" and the other BR classes, but at times the A1s had a tendency to lurch sideways when they hit a bad section of track at speed, unlike the Gresley 2-6-2s or Pacifics, which rode exceptionally well.

Driver Arthur Davis had No. 60149 *Amadis* for some time as his regular locomotive. He was not one to complain, but he did ask one day if the locomotive could be stopped from riding across the fields—at times he was worried that it was not on the lines at all. There was little the depot could do except to tighten up the draw-gear between the engine and tender; this did help a little by using the tender to steady the locomotive.

No. 60157 *Great Eastern* provoked more persistent complaints of instability. This was checked to Peterborough on the "Heart of Midlothian" express and it was found that when the locomotive reached approximately 60 m.p.h. is oscillated continuously from side to side, making it very difficult to fire. The extent of the oscillation was ascertained simply by placing two pieces of coal opposite each other, one on the tender and one on the cab floor, and the total side movement was measured at over 12 in. As soon as the locomotive reached a curve the side oscillation stopped very suddenly, but back on straight track No. 60157 immediately started "crabbing" again. A thorough examination of the engine, including dropping the driving wheels, revealed no defect or feasible remedy, though the design of roller bearing axleboxes fitted to the coupled wheels was found to incorporate a spigot on which the horn face rotated, which probably did not help once the general oscillation started. It was therefore decided to submit a shopping proposal for the locomotive to be further investigated in Doncaster Works. This caused difficulty as No. 60157 was not due for Works attention for a long time and no specific repairs could be itemised. Eventually the Chief Mechanical Engineer's Technical Assistant resident at Doncaster was persuaded to return north on the locomotive following a visit to Top Shed.

No. 60157 was put on the "Tees-Tyne Pullman", which was first stop York, and the driver, Frank Wilson, after being suitably introduced, was advised that if the locomotive did not perform as advertised on this occasion he had better not complain about it

A Down express in December 1961, passing Hatfield. The smoke deflectors are lifting the exhaust clear of the whole train. *(British Railways)*

again. Frank responded with the broadest of winks. The outcome was that No. 60157 was called into Doncaster Works for special examination the very next morning. We learned afterwards that when they hit the points at the south end of New Southgate Station the Chief Mechanical & Electrical Engineer's representative had been ejected from the fireman's seat and thrown across the cab. By the time Hitchin had been reached, he accepted that the point had been proven, but could the driver take it a little steadier to York as he was uncertain they would get there.

On arrival in Doncaster Works No. 60157 was stripped down and all the components examined by the Chief Mechanical Engineer personally. It was concluded there was nothing wrong with the engine and a few days later it returned to King's Cross — riding perfectly. Further enquiries ascertained that the bogie side control springs had been dismantled without being checked and put in the "bosh" for cleaning along with the springs off other locomotives; but whether the same springs had been re-fitted to the locomotive and with the same tension was not recorded.

Whilst No. 60157 was the only A1 at King's Cross to oscillate so badly, others had the occasional tendency to lurch unexpectedly. Further investigation by the design staff at Doncaster revealed that the calculations of the Cartazzi track arrangement under the cab had not allowed for the greater distance between the rear driving wheels and the truck necessitated by the A1's longer grate. One locomotive was later fitted with the recalculated sloping slides, but it was found in practice to make no observable difference.

Most drivers at King's Cross preferred the A4s for their regular locomotives and eventually exchanged A1s for A4s. In the end No. 60156 alone of the twelve A1s was regularly manned by Drivers Duckmanton and McKinley. One day I made a trip to Grantham

No. 60157, a roller bearing Class A1, after putting the fire out on the 10.00 a.m. ex. King's Cross at Barnet. The strum box cock which caused the failure is not visible as it was underneath the well of the tender. *(P. N. Townend)*

A row of Kylchap
Pacifics — two A1s and two
A4s, including *Mallard,* the
world's record holder for
steam. *(P. N. Townend)*

specially to return on this locomotive. At first this alarmed the
driver that he was going to lose his regular engine. I assured him
that this was not the intention, whereupon he came down Stoke at
a very fast rate and the locomotive rode well throughout. The two
crews knew that they had an excellent machine which rarely
needed attention and they kept it all the time the locomotive was
at King's Cross.

Further complaints were made to the Chief Mechanical
Engineer about No. 60136, not because *Alcazar* was a particularly
bad riding locomotive, but because it was recently out of
Doncaster Works after a general overhaul so that its poor riding
could hardly be ascribed to lack of proper maintenance. No.
60136 had a tendency to lurch occasionally, though in between it
rode well. There was a belief that this sensitivity to the track could
possibly be dangerous, although it is only fair to say that no A1
was ever derailed because of its riding qualities. It was decided by
the Chief Mechanical Engineer that No. 60136 should be tested
with indicator shelters in order to take diagrams of the power
produced at each stroke of the piston in the three individual
cylinders. Whilst this could not really have had any connection
with the lurching characteristic, which was not consistent with any
method of working the locomotive, the indicator tests did produce
some interesting results.

No engine had been indicated by Doncaster for over 25 years, so
that these trials were unusual. They ascertained that on this
particular locomotive the indicated horsepower output of the
middle cylinder varied very considerably between the front and

back strokes at the various cut-offs used. This was later found to be due to the expansion of the frames between the outside cylinders and the inside cylinder as the locomotive got hot during the run. Due to the divided drive arrangement, the middle cylinder was well forward of the outside cylinders on the A1, which was not so on the Gresley Pacifics, where all the cylinders were virtually in the same line across the frames, while on the V2 class the three cylinders were actually incorporated in a single casting. It was standard practice at Doncaster to allow for the normal expansion of the valve spindle when setting valves, but in view of what had been revealed it was decided to discontinue this so far as the middle valve was concerned on the A1 class. By this time the A1s were being transferred away again and no further complaints were made by King's Cross, but No. 60136 was finally improved by the fitting of an altered bogie specially made at Doncaster Works.

As already observed, the A1s were extremely economical locomotives. When No. 60114 was almost new in 1949 it had been tested from King's Cross to Grantham and Leeds and had produced an average coal consumption of 40.2 lb. per mile on 490 ton trains and 47.5 lb. per mile on trains of over 600 tons in weight. The average lb. of coal per drawbar horse-power hour consumption throughout the tests was 2.97 on the 490ton trains and 2.83 on the 600ton trains. These were excellent results compared very well with those of the A4s, which produced an average of 3.06 throughout the Interchange Trials of 1948, and 2.92 from A4 No. 60034 on its own East Coast route from King's Cross. The figures recorded with the three double-blastpipe A4s which were used throughout the Interchange Trials were the lowest of any locomotive tested and were obtained on trains approximating to 500 tons in weight. The entire A1 class had been fitted with the Kylchap double exhaust system when built; this feature no doubt helped to achieve the excellent results recorded by the A1s throughout their working life.

Extraordinary liberties were taken with such free-steaming locomotives. For example, on the approach to Peterborough, where there was a long 20 m.p.h. check for many years, the fireman would relax in his seat and steam pressure would be allowed to fall to 150 lb. per sq.in. As soon as the driver opened up the engine again, the fireman would resume firing and by Werrington the boiler pressure would be round to 240 lb. per sq.in. If the earlier Pacifics had been treated in this way it would have been very difficult to recover the situation without losing time. One King's Cross crew working an Up sleeping car express, however, did allow an A1 to get too low in steam and had to come off their train; when the fireman started to pile on the coal as they left Peterborough the remaining fire had got too low and it was put out by the fresh coal. This also happened on several occasions with Leeds men turning round their A1 at Top Shed.

It was always the practice with the wide firebox locomotives to fill the back corners well before leaving the shed, but this could be

Class V2 No. 60881 being coaled at the small tipper coaling plant at King's Cross Station Depot. A Kylchap double chimney is fitted.
(P. N. Townend)

overdone and an excess of fresh coal took time to ignite. Fortunately the A1s were fitted with steam brake, instead of the vacuum brake on the earlier Pacifics, which would not work properly when the engine was very low in steam, as the correct vacuum could not be created. In cases where a heavy fire had not had enough time to ignite properly, the shed pilot would shunt the A1 up and down the yard for a little while to create a draught and finally give it a push in the direction of the outlet signal. The locomotive then dropped down to the station mainly by gravity, but by the time the express was due to leave King's Cross about thirty minutes later the boiler pressure would be round and the locomotive able to climb the 1 in 105 to Holloway without any difficulty.

In the early days of dieselisation the depot had to increase considerably the number of firemen passed for driving so that the large number of drivers required could be released for training on the various diesel locomotive classes. The senior firemen were in the Main Line Lodge Link. Almost overnight all firemen were taken from these links and replaced by junior firemen, many of whom had no experience on Pacifics; some were new to the depot and had never been required previously to work long distances over the East Coast Main Line. It is to their credit that no difficulties ensued. It could not have been done five years earlier without a serious effect on timekeeping, but by the time the crew changes were made most of the Top Shed Pacifics had been fitted with the Kylchap double blastpipes and the considerable experience required to get the best out of the earlier Pacifics was no longer vital.

One day I accompanied a young lad recently transferred on promotion from Canklow on an A1 locomotive and asked how he found working on the Pacifics over such long distances as King's Cross to Newcastle. He replied that it was an easy day's work, as he could sit down for over half the journey—"but you couldn't do that with a 'Black 5' or a 'Crab' from Somers Town to Masborough; then you knew you'd done a day's work," he added. One morning in 1958 a roller-bearing A1 No. 60157 *Great Eastern* was beautifully turned out—or so it was thought—to work the 10.00 a.m. "Flying Scotsman" to Newcastle. But it came to a stand at New Barnet, and the enormous fire the fireman had built up had to be put out on the track to avoid dropping the lead plugs. Both injectors had failed. They had not been entirely free of trouble on any of the various classes of Pacific; but around this time a number of serious delays occurred due to failure of the injectors to put the water required into the boiler. After exhaustive investigation we found that there was little if anything wrong with the injectors themselves. The trouble lay in the feed supply from the tenders.

No. 60157 was hauled back to the shed. There it was found that whilst it had been in Works a few weeks earlier the opportunity had been taken to modify the tender and fit a strumbox underneath the tender well. This addition had become fashionable on

BR Standard locomotives, but it was completely alien to LNER locomotive tenders. The strumbox incorporated a filter plate consisting of many small diameter holes in a flat plate and a stop cock, so that the feed supply could be shut off to enable the plate to be removed for cleaning without the need to empty the tank, which was necessary with the previous LNER practice of fitting "top hat" sieves over the individual feed supply pipes inside the tank. All that was wrong with No. 60157 was that the cock had closed and no water could pass to the injectors. This cock had worked to the shut position with the vibration of the locomotive in running along the track and no one had noticed the cock was closed.

The strumboxes on BR Standard tenders were external and could be seen, but on the Pacific tenders they were almost inaccessible between the frames under the tender well and no one at the depot was aware that tenders were being fitted with them. In order to prevent the stop cock closing again a locking plate was fitted to the square on the cock spindle, but the occasional injector failure on the road continued to occur with no readily apparent reason. So the sieve plate was carefully examined and now it was found that the small holes quickly became blocked or reduced in size due to algae and other detritus picked up from the water troughs, which the Top Shed Pacifics used very considerably on the East Coast main line. The sieve plates were therefore removed completely, but after another heavy delay with an A1 on the Up "Flying Scotsman" at Hatfield—which received a mention in the Sunday newspapers—further detailed investigations were made.

The King's Cross Inspector who was on the locomotive when it had failed reported that no difficulty had been experienced from Newcastle until they were approaching Hatfield, when the second injector was put on. Neither injector would then work and the fire had to be quickly dropped. Afterwards there was no difficulty in getting either injector to work. Both injectors were fed through the same hole in the strumbox, which was about 2½ in. diameter, and the single feedcock opened about 1½ in. Sufficient water could not be passed through this aperture to keep both injectors operating on a Pacific working hard, particularly when the tender tank water level was reduced to a low level. Ironically it was the Kylchap-fitted Pacifics that usually failed, as the boiler would still steam with both injectors on. No difficulty was experienced if only one injector at a time was used.

A simple test was arranged to demonstrate the problem. Two full 5,000 gal. tenders, one with a strumbox fitted and the other one with the normal LNER separate feed arrangement to each injector, were uncoupled from their locomotives and stood alongside each other in the shed. The tender tanks were both filled and then the feed valves were fully opened on each tender at the same time. The water from the tender with the standard LNER arrangement shot out several feet, but the water from the other

One of the last steam locomotives to visit Top Shed after the depot had closed, No. 4472 restored to LNER livery under the coaling plant but being coaled out of wagon. *(P. N. Townend)*

tender, particularly when the water level was reduced, only just emerged from the outlet of the feed pipes.

There was no reasonable way of increasing the size of the orifice in the strumbox. The cock was therefore removed altogether and it was found that a heavy hammer dropped from a suitable height made a very adequate-sized hole in the strumbox casting. At the same time the individual tender feed valves to each injector operated by the fireman were carefully aligned and enlarged. Thereafter the abnormal run of injector failures subsided to a very low level and serious injector failures became a rarity; but the strumboxes had become empty boxes and no longer served any purpose.

The considerable extension of through engine workings in 1956-57 resulted eventually in an extension of the regular engine roster from 9 to 17 locomotives, shared by the 34 drivers now in the No. 1 Link. The allocation of Pacifics to Top Shed reached a peak of 42 for a short time in the Autumn of 1957, before reductions over the following years—initially because the depot could not handle such large numbers, but later as the diesels commenced to work over the East Coast Main Line.

Many of the additional workings required Top Shed Pacifics and men to travel through to Newcastle and lodge before returning the following day, whereas for some years previously the "Tees-Tyne Pullman" had been the only such daily working. The 10.00 a.m. "Flying Scotsman", which New Egland Depot had covered with the Thompson A2 varieties off the Up "Aberdonian" to Grantham, became a King's Cross lodge turn to Newcastle, and also both the morning and afternoon "Talisman" services. The 266 Down express freight train from King's Cross Goods to Niddrie, to quote its number in the Working Time Table, became

a No. 1 Link lodge turn to Newcastle. With the benefit of the alterations made to the Pacifics, the through engine workings were completely successful and remained in operation until the end of steam traction at the depot.

The working of 266 Down each afternoon became probably the hardest of the Newcastle turns, as it involved about seven hours' work on the road, somewhat longer than the four and a half hours of an express passenger train. At York the enginemen were booked for a short break and the coal was thrown forward on the tender by a relief crew whilst the train was being examined. Punctuality was exemplary, no doubt aided by the fact that the booked arrival time at Newcastle just enabled the crew to enjoy well-earned refreshment before closing time. The driver's regular engine was turned out each day cleaned as if it was to take one of the after-noon named trains — indeed the return working the following day was on an express. 266 Down was usually heavily loaded, generally between 50 and 60 four-wheeled wagons. Although it was booked to depart at 3.05 p.m. and to average 50 m.p.h. between stops, no maximum speed was laid down for the wagons at that time and some of the Top Link crews took advantage of this to see how far they could get down the main line before they were turned from main to slow to let the 4.0 p.m. "Talisman" pass. The train was formed of four-wheeled wagons, many of which had to be put off *en route* as they ran hot or dropped the brake gear; it was not unusual to reduce the load by four or five to Doncaster in this way, but nevertheless a well-known driver did one day succeed in reaching Retford before being turned off the main line.

The year 1958 was the beginning of the end at Top Shed, for it saw the first five English Electric 2,000 h.p. Type 4 diesel-electric

Class A4 No. 60028 *Walter K. Whigham* waiting to leave King's Cross No. 10 platform with the LNER Royal Train, June 1961. *(P. N. Townend)*

locomotives arrive to commence passenger service on the main line. In the spring of 1959 the North British 1,000 h.p., English Electric Deltic 1,100 h.p., and BRCW Sulzer 1,160 h.p. Type 2s were beginning to take over the suburban work from the N2s and L1s but all were too heavy to work over Blackfriars Bridge to the Southern Region lines. It was another two years before the Derby-built Sulzer 2s, fitted with smaller boilers and lightened in weight, arrived to replace the Hornsey J50s. The N2s and L1s, however, substituted for the diesels considerably in the early years and the drivers usually had a go at keeping time with them. Later, the B1s were also found to be able to deputise for the Brush 2s. The performance of the North British Type 2s was particularly poor and on the 17.39 ex King's Cross, loaded to nine, they were likened to an L1 short of steam.

Due to the improvements made in detail to the Pacifics as described earlier in this chapter, remarkably little difficulty was experienced at Top Shed in covering the main line services during the prolonged transitional period. It was indeed fortunate that this necessary betterment of the steam locomotives had been made late in the day, particularly the fitting of the Kylchap exhaust system. The results proved the small cost incurred to have been well worthwhile, as the Pacific locomotives at Top Shed succeeded in attaining a standard of performance and an intensity of working when required that had not previously been achieved. Both A3s and A4s substituted for the English Electric Co. Type 4s day after day as necessary to Newcastle, returning in the diesel diagram. On some days only the Pullman workings to Sheffield were covered by a Type 4 and all the harder Newcastle diagrams were covered by steam.

When long-distance workings to Newcastle had become the

Below left: The demolition of the Coaling Plant in 1964. The hopper weighed 1,400 tons and was demolished by explosives. *(British Railways)*

Below right: The demolition of the Water Softening Plant in 1967. The brick building remains in use to house a small water treatment plant. *(British Railways)*

normal practice again in 1956-57, the locomotives were booked to stand over and return with the same crews after lodging. There had been no previous attempt to run Pacifics there and back in a little over 12 hours for the round trip as was laid down in the diesel diagrams. No difficulty was experienced in doing so now, and if required an A4 would be off on another round working to Newcastle within a few hours of having completed the previous trip. It was no longer necessary to have the fire out after every working beyond Doncaster; this was solely due to the Kylchap exhaust system and a bit of insurance thrown in with the firebox powder. Some locomotives did not have the fire out for a week and performance did not suffer. The Deltics had additionally arrived on the main line in 1960, but in one four-week period of 1961 it was an A4 which ran 11,800 miles — the highest mileage of any locomotive, Deltics and Type 4s included, in that month.

In September 1961 the "Elizabethan" completed the world's longest non-stop run to Edinburgh and back for the last time. Appropriately, the world's record-holder for steam traction, No. 60022 *Mallard* of Top Shed, worked the Down train.

In June 1961, for the occasion of the wedding of the Duke of Kent and Katherine Worsley in York Minster, three special trains, with a fourth standing by, were scheduled from King's Cross to York and back in the day for the wedding guests, including the Queen, the whole of the Royal Family, the Queen Mother, and many other important State officials. The decision was made at the highest level in the Region that all the trains would be worked by steam. Top Shed turned out No. 60028 on the former LNER Royal Train for the Queen and Royal Family, Nos. 60003 and 60015 for the guests, and No. 60014 to stand pilot. All the engines were turned out immaculately and No. 60028 had the cab roof painted white. All completed the round workings without any difficulty and arrived back at King's Cross before time, despite late starts from York; one last "ton" was said to have been achieved down Stoke with one of the trains carrying the guests. The General Manager, watching the first train away from King's Cross, said that even he could see the locomotives were turned out in excellent condition which he could not do with the diesels. Although that summarised the feelings at the time, the Sulzer 2,750 h.p. locomotives entered service in 1962 and at the commencement of the summer service on June 16 1963, Top Shed was finally closed. All scheduled steam workings to King's Cross ceased, although the odd steam locomotive still arrived at King's Cross occasionally from the North when substituting for a failed Deltic. Late in 1964, No. 60106 *Flying Fox* arrived on the Up "Flying Scotsman" for the last time, creditably booked only 2 min. "due to loco" on the "Deltic" schedule then in force, and having run over 2,600,000 miles since being built in 1923.

The buildings at Top Shed were demolished soon after closure. Standing afterwards on the levelled site, it was impossible to realise that one of the most important steam depots in the country had once occupied such a small area of land.

Class A3 No. 60066 framed in an arch of the original engine stables with the rear of the rebuilt main-line shed in the background. For many years a traverser occupied the area where the two Pacifics are standing, and the main line shed was dead-ended on all except one road. *(C. R. L. Coles)*

Allocation of the London Division at January 1922, GNR Depot Code 3

Class	Load Class	Running Nos.	Total
J21	E	1, 2, 3, 7, 10, 11, 12	7
D1	W	41, 42, 49, 50, 56, 1321, 1322, 1337, 1377, 1389, 1391	11
J4	B	342, 384, 387, 717, 1099, 1100, 1136, 1137, 1139, 1169, 1170	11
J5	B	101, 302, 313, 314, 373, 383, 385, 641, 642, 716, 745, 834, 844, 1036, 1037, 1088, 1138	17
J14	F	111, 921, 922, 923, 925, 926, 927, 961, 964, 969, 970, 971, 972, 974, 975, 976, 979, 1046, 1047, 1048, 1050, 1051, 1054, 1056, 1057, 1058, 1059, 1060, 1212-5	32
J15	F	675, 676, 785, 786, 855, 857, 901, 909, 910, 139a	10
J16	H	473a	1
J17	F	612, 615	2
J18	F	684, 685, 686, 687, 144a, 149a	6
J22	A	539, 574, 584, 585	4
J13	H	1204, 1227-34, 1240, 1251-3, 1255, 1256, 1261, 1262, 1275, 1281, 1282, 1285	21
L1	N	117, 125, 137, 151, 154, 156	6
N1	F	190, 1551-3, 1555, 1557-9, 1561-3, 1565, 1567, 1570, 1571, 1573, 1575-86, 1588, 1589, 1591, 1596-1605	41
C1	Z	252, 253, 254, 274, 277, 278, 279, 299, 301, 949, 1400, 1411, 1426, 1427, 1428, 1440-4, 1450, 1458-61	25
G1	M	767, 770, 931	3
D3	W	1072, 1073, 1078, 1080, 1312, 1314, 1346	7
C2	M	1534, 1537, 1541, 1548, 1550	5

Class	Load Class	Running Nos.	Total
N2	F	1606-15, 1721-70	*60*
H2	E.1	1632	*1*
H3	E.1	1641, 1645, 1649, 1651, 1653-6, 1666-9, 1671, 1674, 1679	*15*
Steam Motors		5, 8	*2*

Note. GNR Locomotive classification used   *Total*   *287*

Allocation of King's Cross Depot, BR Shed Code 34A at 20th April 1958

LNER Class	BR Class	BR Engine Nos	Total
Class A4	8 P	60003, 60006, 60007, 60008, 60010, 60013, 60014, 60015, 60017, 60021, 60022, 60025, 60026, 60028, 60029, 60030, 60032, 60033, 60034	*19*
Class A1	8 P	60119, 60122, 60128, 60139, 60149, 60156, 60157, 60158	*8*
Class A3	7 P	60039, 60044, 60055, 60059, 60062, 60066, 60103, 60108, 60110	*9*
Class V2	6 MT	60800, 60814, 60820, 60854, 60862, 60871, 60902, 60903, 60914, 60950, 60983	*11*
Class B1	5 MT	61075, 61139, 61200, 61331, 61364, 61393, 61394	*7*
Class L1	4 MTT	67757, 67768, 67770, 67773, 67774, 67776, 67779, 67784, 67793, 67794, 67797	*11*
Class J52	3 FT	68831, 68862	*2*
	5	73157, 73158, 73159	*3*
Class N2	3 MTT	69490, 69491, 69492, 69493, 69495, 69496, 69497, 69498, 69499, 69506, 69512, 69516, 69517, 69520, 69521, 69523, 69524, 69526, 69527, 69528, 69529, 69532, 69535, 69536, 69538, 69539, 69540, 69541, 69542, 69543, 69544, 69545, 69546, 69548, 69549, 69568, 69569, 69570, 69571, 69573, 69574, 69575, 69576, 69577, 69578, 69579, 69580, 69581, 69583, 69584, 69585, 69589, 69591, 69592, 69593	*55*
			125

Also 23 Diesel-Electric Shunting Locomotives   *23*